ENGAGING THE VOICE OF WISDOM

A GUIDE FOR BETTER DECISION-MAKING

TJIKKO Publishing
2501 N. Harwood Street, Suite 2001, Dallas, Texas 75201
tjikko.com

ISBN: 978-0-9909753-3-5
eISBN: 978-0-9909753-5-9

For all bearers of light

We are not provided with wisdom, we must discover it for ourselves,
after a journey through the wilderness which no one else can take for us,
an effort which no one can spare us.
— Marcel Proust, *In Search of Lost Time, Vol II* (1913–27)

There are two varieties of wisdom: ordinary wisdom, which we grasp with the mind and express in words and concepts; and an eternal wisdom, which courses through the center of our being and *knows* what is right. This work presents the first type of wisdom to help you rediscover the second.

Contents

Introduction

Only you can answer the most important questions in life, whether they involve your health, relationships, vocation, avocations, or the choices you make for those who rely on you. And as those moments arrive, no one else can tell you which principles to uphold, when to yield for the sake of harmony, or if it is time to let go with grace. Yet here is a truth we often come to understand only with time: Every decision matters. Each casts its shadow or light, in ways subtle or plain to see, across the landscape of your life. Some fall like a veil of darkness, immediate and unmistakable. Others dawn like the sunrise, their brilliance revealed gradually with time.

How, then, can we ensure we choose wisely?

This exploration of choice builds upon themes I first examined in *The Power of 10*, a book centered on inquiry and questions of meaning, such as *Who am I?* and *How do I influence others? The Power of 10* encouraged readers to set intentions (or advocacies) for *living into* one's potential, in essence, becoming your greatest self. While that book explored the importance of articulating a purpose and guiding principles — what economists might call the *macro* — it did not fully address the *micro*: how to apply them to the myriad decisions we encounter day-to-day.

Consider this: You have set an intention to embody kindness. But what happens when you encounter someone behaving offensively or violating social norms? A person stepping in front of people standing in a line, interrupting or talking over others, or taking credit for someone else's work. Do you let the matter go, believing the behavior is a temporary lapse in judgment or the person is unaware of social norms? Or do you intervene, knowing that allowing such behavior may do a disservice not only to the person but also to the larger community?

While *The Power of 10* prompts us to periodically contemplate the questions of a lifetime to guide how we live each day, this work asks us to consider the questions we encounter each day that, together, determine the course of a life. And the result? A life of purpose and meaning, or one marked by missed opportunities and the weight of regret.

For Those Who Dare to Choose

This book is for the strivers, the seekers, and the visionaries. Those who not only hold the potential to make the world a better place but often do: some through quiet acts of kindness that transform a single life, others through bold feats that uplift many. These are individuals who hold themselves to the highest standards, driven by an inner resolve to improve, and guided by a sense of purpose — perhaps an ideal so vast it may take more than a lifetime to fully realize.

In a word, this book is for anyone committed to living deliberately — choicefully.

You may be only beginning to recognize your capabilities, or you may have already achieved what others consider success. Yet even the most capable among us remain vulnerable to doubt. At times, the questions before us loom larger than the answers we hold. Other times, the way forward seems obscured, just beyond the edges of our perception. In these moments, you may ask, *Who can I turn to for guidance?* or *How do I begin to make the right choice?*

Each of us benefits from an experienced guide. That is the purpose of this book: to serve as a trusted companion in moments of uncertainty, whether you are weighing a decision that may alter the rhythm of a day or hold the potential to redraw the map of a life. Whatever the stakes, this book offers both philosophical reflection and practical guidance to help you move forward with clarity and confidence.

Fair warning, though: The pursuit of wisdom is no easy course. It requires restraint when instinct urges you to react, trusting your intuition rather than giving into convention, and harnessing curiosity, compassion, or creativity to respond in a manner that is *right* rather than expedient. Such a pursuit calls for courage, honest self-reflection, and a steadfast commitment to improvement. It requires confronting your limitations and transcending them. Yet the rewards are far-reaching, extending into every facet of life and creating the foundation for a meaningful existence.

If you seek to exercise your agency with purpose and resolve, then this work is for you. Consider this book both an invitation for today and a gift to your future self, one that may ultimately lead to wisdom and enlightenment.

Weaving Wisdom into Everyday Life

By day, I work in business and co-lead a private investment firm. As part of my role, I serve as an active board member of the companies we invest in. Given the nature of my responsibilities, decision-making is a critical aspect of my work. From evaluating which companies to invest in to overseeing how those investments are managed, my choices can directly or indirectly influence hundreds, sometimes thousands, of people. This responsibility has instilled in me a profound sense of duty to evaluate each choice with care.

But why do I emphasize wisdom over the traditional hallmarks of a rigorous process, such as analysis, logic, or reasoning? While these form the foundation of sound decision-making, wisdom reaches beyond analytical reasoning alone. It draws on truth, virtue, and discernment, uniting the measurable and the immeasurable, the rational and the ethical, the seen and the unseen. It ensures that decisions are not only well-reasoned but also farsighted and just. For this reason, I have pursued wisdom throughout my life, driven not only by professional obligation but by a personal need.

That need began in solitude.

I have often felt alone in making decisions, uncertain whether to trust my voice. During my formative years, my parents were largely absent or distracted, and we lived far from any extended family. Our home did not echo with the presence of a grandparent, uncle, aunt, or any surrogate to consult. Moreover, I was, and remain, an only child. So where was I to turn for guidance?

In effect, when describing who this book is for, it is for anyone who has known this same sense of aloneness, in any part of life, without a trusted presence to turn to.

While I firmly believe we all have an innate sense of right and wrong, I wanted to find a more encompassing moral philosophy, something against which to measure my decisions. I turned first to the diverse teachings of Abrahamic religions, whose compelling narratives distill lessons on ethics and the complexities of the human experience. (Why else would generations keep reading them? The themes, storylines, and dialogues all hint at life's enduring secrets.) I then explored metaphysics, epistemology, logic, and the nature of consciousness. My inquiry then broadened to the field of psychology, probing the influences of culture, myth, and archetype, along with theories on adult development, including integral theory, constructive developmental theory, and research specifically focused on wisdom.[1]

Throughout this exploration, I kept a notebook, loftily entitled *Universal Truths*. In it, I recorded notable quotes and excerpts from various sources and generated tables and charts. I compiled lists of common traits attributed to individuals perceived as wise or adept at decision-making. While the volume eventually grew to hundreds of pages, revealing numerous insights into the human experience, this work remained largely theoretical. As the proverb reminds us: "The map is not the territory."[2] Over time, I could trace a line from Descartes's rationalism and the Enlightenment's emphasis on reason and autonomy to Sartre's existentialist metaphysics and its focus on subjective freedom. But I still lacked guidance on everyday matters, such as choosing between two enticing job offers or deciding whether wearing sneakers with a suit was fashion forward or a sartorial misstep.[3]

The real shift occurred when I redirected my efforts, away from identifying answers for achieving the ideal life and toward understanding which questions to ask in order to create it. Or, to return to the map analogy: If life stretches toward the horizon, then rather than continue surveying familiar terrain, my task became constructing a compass for exploration. I revisited the teachings of religion, philosophy, and science, viewing them both as subjects for retrospective analysis and as tools for prospective evaluation. Seen in this way, principles from diverse sources such as the Eightfold Path of Buddhism, Stoic philosophy, and the scientific method, each contribute their wisdom, helping us make better decisions amid the choices we encounter every day.

And how did this quest influence my life? As I began writing, I sat down to reflect on a number of personal choices made over time. A few of these appear within the text. Indeed, any reconciliation of my past reveals a life dotted with poor decisions. As Hermann Hesse aptly described, my experience has not been "sweet and harmonious like invented stories. It tastes of folly and confusion, of madness and dreams — like the lives of all those who no longer want to deceive themselves."[4] Nonetheless, in the final accounting, I hope the scale will tip toward more good choices — even if, alone, we can never truly measure the balance.

What becomes apparent upon reflection, however, is how frequently I recall myself reacting impulsively rather than responding in a conscious, thoughtful manner. Or how I allowed others, circumstances, or the mere passage of time to make decisions for me. While I could offer a variety of reasons for these lapses, the root causes could often be traced back to two primary sources. The first involves purposeful ignorance, moments where I deliberately disregarded the information available at that time. The second is defiance, when, even aware of the right decision, I prioritized immediate, unhealthy gratification over enduring, wholesome satisfaction. Ultimately, we often do know whether we are making the *right* decision.

This same line of inquiry also led me to wonder why anyone would want to read a book on decision-making from someone who has made their fair share of poor choices. That is a reasonable question. Yet the lessons I have learned have compelled me to become more intentional, and ideally, more skillful, as a decision-maker today. By sharing the practices outlined in this book, I hope to help others avoid some of the missteps I have made.

Regardless of your chosen direction, whether it is the seven steps described in the pages ahead or one you devise, know this: *You are not alone.* Each step you take toward self-development, in becoming healthier, happier, and more successful, benefits not only you but us all. This is the essence of wisdom. Thus, each person who engages in its pursuit, practice, and participation contributes to the collective good. Through this ongoing effort, we will create a better world. Together.

Three Premises

The practice described in this book rests on three essential premises:

1. As humans, we are capable of making choices.
2. Our bodies and hearts, in concert with our minds, are sources of wisdom.
3. Consistently making the right choices leads to a better life.

For the first premise, we must accept that our lives are not steered solely by fate, destiny, or divine will: that we hold both the capacity and responsibility to choose. Consider a simple test: Can you decide whether to continue reading (or listening to) this book? If your answer is affirmative, we can agree that this premise holds, even in a hypothetical universe where the concept of choice is ultimately an illusion.

The second premise rests on the belief that we can improve how we make choices. It suggests that decision-making is a skill, not a random or purely innate process. Like any skill, it can be refined through intention and practice, drawing upon more than logical reasoning or adherence to any fixed algorithm. Our bodies and hearts offer insights our minds might overlook. The body signals emotional states and levels of comfort or unease. The heart points us toward compassion, urging us to relieve suffering and respond with care. By fostering a more holistic approach — listening to these three sources of wisdom: body, heart, and mind — and learning from our experiences, we can hone the skills needed to make better decisions across all areas of life.

Finally, the third premise posits that making the right choices is the most direct path to the life you desire. Here, a *right* choice is one guided by good intentions, mindful of the well-being of yourself and others, suited to the circumstances, and guided by wisdom. Many readers are focused on financial success or professional achievement, and understandably so, because such accomplishments often provide stability and opportunities. Yet if you are like most people, you also seek a life enriched by good health, meaningful relationships, and lasting contentment. By learning to pause, seek perspective, and engage your voice of wisdom rather than merely reacting, your choices will more closely align with your intentions and aspirations, leading to a more fulfilling life.

Throughout this work, we will touch on two important concepts: *intentions* and *aspirations*. Alongside our choices, these ideals influence the course of our lives. Aspirations point to where we are going: our long-term goals and dreams. They express what we are aiming to achieve. Intentions, by contrast, represent the *how*: the values, principles, or standards we commit to upholding along the way. (It is worth noting that intentions may spring from or be the product of your personal moral code, a subject we will explore in greater detail later.) Together, these forces offer both direction and guidance across our personal and professional lives.

A Challenge — or Two

At the end of each chapter, alongside a summary and questions designed to help you absorb the material, you will find a set of challenges, Self-Discovery and Further Exploration, intended to bring the chapter's central lessons into practice. The Self-Discovery challenges are individual exercises that promote a richer understanding of your decision-making process. The Further Exploration challenges involve conversations with others, offering insight into how they approach questions of truth and rightness. Responding to these prompts may take as little as fifteen or twenty minutes, or unfold over longer periods, inviting reflection on the nature of wisdom and the decision-making process itself. The final chapter introduces an additional challenge, envisioned as a lifelong pursuit, echoing the seven-step process itself.

The goal of these challenges is not perfection but progress. Be patient with yourself as you work through them, and if you find yourself at an impasse, you can call on the three C's, the natural abodes of wisdom: *curiosity, compassion,* and *creativity*. These inherent capacities are channels to the voice of wisdom within us. Curiosity opens our minds and provides the energy to ask questions. Compassion opens the heart to others and differing perspectives. Creativity ignores perceived limitations to imagine a better way.

Most importantly, as you move from reading these pages to living the process, remember that the true value of this approach lies beyond memorizing its content. Rather, it resides in applying the process to the questions you confront each day, from what to eat for your next meal to whether to change careers. Put simply: Life itself is the place of practice. And any real practice requires active engagement. Just as you cannot truly learn to dance the salsa without standing up, moving your body, and syncing with the rhythm, you cannot fully absorb this material without participation.

Now is the time to step toward wisdom. To begin this pursuit is to choose with intention: to pause before each decision, turn inward, and listen. With each right choice, you advance one step closer to the sacred fire, the living body of wisdom carried forward from one life to another across generations. This is not a task that can be completed in a day or even a decade. It is a lifelong pursuit, one that asks much of you but offers much in return, not only for yourself but for those around you. In taking up this challenge, you will inevitably find yourself becoming not only healthier, happier, and more successful but also wiser. And in time, you, too, will become a bearer of light.

Fiat lux.

Chapter 1 — Why Wisdom?

Where is the wisdom we have lost in knowledge?
Where is the knowledge we have lost in information?
—T. S. Eliot[5]

Of all the stars to guide your course through life, why choose wisdom?

The word *wisdom* can be used in various ways and perceived differently across cultures. Western culture often associates wisdom with empirical knowledge, rationality, and critical thinking, strongly emphasizing logic and the scientific method. In contrast, Eastern ideals of wisdom often emphasize harmony, balance, and interconnectedness, focusing more on morality and ethics to encourage virtues like compassion and humility, integrating emotional understanding with cognitive insight.

From a philosophical standpoint, wisdom involves mastering the dialectics that define human existence, from the mundane to the transcendental. This includes reconciling dichotomies like good versus bad, control versus surrender, and selfishness versus selflessness. Or as Socratic questioning might posit: How do we discern good from bad amid moral ambiguities? How do we balance independence and our dependence on others? Can we align selfish desires with altruistic needs? Such questions challenge us to consider whether logic and reasoning alone suffice or if ethics and equanimity are also needed to attain wisdom. Alternatively, as ancient Eastern philosophies suggest, there might be a middle way to integrate both for a more comprehensive understanding.

What we *can* take away from these broader views of wisdom is that (1) irrespective of cultural context, wisdom includes the concept of self-transcendence, and (2) because every question generates new questions and each choice opens up myriad perspectives, wisdom represents the endpoint of human development. Our focus here, however, is more practical: how to call on wisdom to help us make better choices in our daily lives. Therefore, in the context of our discussion, wisdom can be described as *a quality of discernment, the ability to perceive what is true and right, coupled with an inclination to pursue it.*

By unraveling its layers of meaning, we encounter the threefold nature of wisdom. First, wisdom enables us to *perceive* what is *true* — *reality*. Specifically, it points to what reasonable minds agree on based on existing facts and information. While the past can provide us with experience, experience alone is insufficient; it only suggests what may have been true under a particular set of circumstances. If there is one enduring, capital-T truth, it is this: *Everything changes.* What may have been true in the past may not be true today.

Consider your life. The person you are now might feel markedly different from who you were even yesterday. Your outlook, desires, and even tastes have likely evolved. Extend this timeline over a year or a decade, and the transformation becomes even more apparent. You are indeed a changed and changing individual. Hence, the importance of guarding against overreliance on past experiences and instead continuously reassessing what holds true in the present.

Second, wisdom aids us in *conceiving* what is *right*. The distinction between true and right is an important one. While truth tells us *what is*, right points to what *could be*. In other words, right suggests the optimal course of action given current circumstances. While it may be true that we are filling our oceans with plastics, is it right?

Undoubtedly not.

Third, wisdom honors your free will or agency to choose, providing the *inclination* to act on what is right. However, simply knowing what to do — and you will *know* — is not enough. Consider the distinct feeling you had the last time you recognized the importance of taking a stand for an unpopular viewpoint as the right thing to do, yet you remained silent out of fear or disapproval. That sense of knowing, coupled with the regret of inaction, is wisdom calling you to act. Even if the veracity of the choice may have been obscured in the moment, had you instead spoken up, the wisdom behind that decision would have eventually become apparent over time.

It is in pausing to assess what is true and right, and integrating these insights into our thoughts, words, and actions, when wisdom truly comes to life. Wisdom guides us through the countless choices we encounter at any moment, from where to place our attention to what we say, the tone in which we say it, and the actions we undertake. By making better choices, wisdom ensures that we not only survive as a species but also thrive as individuals, becoming healthy, happy, successful, and, ideally, loving beings.

We Need Wisdom More than Ever

Wisdom is not a new concept but a timeless ideal extolled in nearly every culture. Humanity has been urged to seek wisdom for thousands of years. The Bhagavad Gita, the Dhammapada, the Qur'an, and the Bible all sound this call.[6] Wisdom, each extolls, is more valuable than any treasure. Pursue, practice, and participate through sharing, they advise. As the Book of Proverbs, a foundational text for all Abrahamic faiths that centers on intentions, moral behavior, and the meaning of human life, commands: "Get wisdom; get insight . . . Do not forsake her, and she will keep you; love her, and *she* will guard you."[7] However, the virtues of wisdom lie not solely within the province of religion.

Wisdom is equally revered in the realms of philosophy and science. The word *philosophy* itself is derived from the Greek *philosophia* or love of wisdom.[8] Philosophers — by definition, lovers of wisdom — suggest it nourishes our hunger for knowledge. Scientists, too, propose that wisdom catalyzes humanity's biological imperative to evolve and adapt.[9] We are, after all, *Homo sapiens* — wise humans.

While religion, philosophy, and science highlight the merits of wisdom, its most enduring influence lies in its practical application to contemporary life. Our need for wisdom is urgent.

Not only is the world becoming more complex, but it is also changing at a fantastic speed. A person born just a few generations ago would hardly recognize the hyperconnected, super-stimulated, better-faster-now world. We live in an era where efficacy is valued over carefulness and impatience is rewarded over devotion, and we are overwhelmed with choices. According to some researchers, we are required to make more than ten thousand decisions a day.[10] As a result, many of us feel inundated by an onslaught of new information and external symbols. With so much pressure to produce quick results, it may seem like a luxury, perhaps even neglectful, to ignore a mountain of tasks waiting to be accomplished while we pause to contemplate an approach.

We generate more information in a day than existed in the first two thousand years following the invention of paper. Yet, even with all the information at our fingertips, making any decision can feel overwhelming. At any moment, we can read about the experiences, opinions, and analyses of millions of others. You might expect that access to this knowledge would make it easier to decide what running shoes to buy, where to go on vacation, or which retirement plan to choose, but the opposite is true. Despite all the available choices, we often feel adrift in a sea of uncertainty, apprehensive about what the future might hold, longing for a simpler life.

Meanwhile, the world has become a noisy place. Machines around us continuously pulse, whir, and hum. Your phone, unconstrained, incessantly beeps and buzzes. Technology is transforming how people work, think, and connect with our cultural values. We live amid a rushing stream of signals where our actions and words have potential global reach, yet we allocate little time to processing information and engaging in thoughtful dialogue, collaborative ideation, experimentation, or creativity. We know more about each other's external daily lives than ever before, but we spend less time relaxing together or allowing space for those quiet moments that enable us to absorb the thoughtful traces of individuals' inner lives.

And what of free time? Conditioned in this way to an endless stream of distraction, we fill the void with news, music, or entertainment. The reality is that the noise will never subside. If anything, the volume will inevitably grow louder.

Reconnecting to the Wisdom Within

The solution — or rather, the antidote — is to reconnect with the voice of wisdom, that quiet, still voice within us: *a confluence of knowledge, experience, and insight flowing through all living beings.* This wisdom exists in each of us irrespective of age, occupation, or personal circumstances. Passed from generation to generation as part of our collective inheritance, wisdom is the part of us that *knows*. Even if it never utters a word, the voice of wisdom expresses itself through our bodies, hearts, and minds.

No matter how crowded our attention may become, the voice of wisdom is always accessible. All it requires is for us to pause, take a breath, and turn inward. Doing so allows us to reconnect with the silent space at the center of our being. It is here that we can access the wisdom within to guide us with insight and understanding.

Absent careful choice, we react. Sometimes, it is out of fear or an instinct to survive. Or we start from a place of believing that we already know, relying on answers from the past when we do not. Even if we attempt to ignore it, the voice of wisdom makes itself known. We might perceive it as a feeling, an instinct, intuition, an inkling, a sixth sense, or a firmly held conviction in our hearts. Or it may present itself as a whisper sheltered in the quiet stillness within us, suggesting what is called for in the moment — for ourselves, for others, and the environment around us. And it all starts with one moment. One decision. One act, guided by wisdom.

Better Decision-Making Is a Skill Anyone Can Learn

Conventional thinking suggests that wisdom is a function of age, intellect, or experience. While each may contribute to its formation, none of these factors alone produce wisdom in isolation. Many older people never reach their potential. Intelligent individuals make foolish choices. And, despite experience, almost everyone finds themselves ensnared in recurring unhealthy patterns.

Nor is there a correlation between the modern ideal of success and wisdom. Although society often judges a person's value based on popularity, influence, or wealth, wisdom cannot be purchased. Otherwise, every wealthy person would be healthy, happy, and wise. However, we know this is far from reality. History, mythology, and popular culture provide plenty of examples of wealthy yet unwise individuals, from King Midas to the various celebrity, political, and business icons who make monumental mistakes, ending up unhappy, broke, or both.

This is not to suggest that we should disregard the advice of professionals or individuals with specialized knowledge. People consult doctors, lawyers, and teachers for a reason. However, it is equally important to consider their advice within its given context. A doctor can prescribe a course of physical therapy but must rely on you to gauge how much strain to exert during each session, because only you know your body's limits. A lawyer can advise you on the potential merits of a legal action but cannot determine the level of risk you are willing to undertake. A teacher can instruct you on the correct pronunciation of *je t'aime* in French, but only you can discern when and to whom you offer these words.

Making good decisions is a skill anyone can practice and improve, whether you are eight or eighty-eight. A fundamental misunderstanding often arises when we consider decision-making a soft skill we absorb over time. Just as consistent practice on the piano, with focus and determination, leads to improvement, the same holds for conscious decision-making. This principle explains why symphonies rehearse, pilots train in simulators, and doctors attend morbidity and mortality conferences.

Consider an aspect of your life: your health, education, relationships, work, finances, or any area that is prominent for you right now. Perhaps there is a subject your mind revisits or one that interferes with your sleep. Recall a few significant choices you have made in this area of your life. How many of those resulted from careful deliberation, where you paused to clarify what was at stake, considered multiple points of view, and opted for the healthy, loving, joyous expression of a thought, word, or action? And how many resulted from impulse, habit, or prevailing emotions? The answer might be more of the latter than you would like to admit.

Now ask yourself: What was the value of each of those good choices? Priceless, perhaps. Conversely, what has been the cost of one bad choice? Your approach to decision-making would likely differ if you knew the stakes were higher. But how would you know?

Herein lies the mystery. Some choices may affect a day in your life, others an entire lifetime. Sometimes, the most seemingly insignificant decisions determine our fate.

Take, for example, the decision to accept an offer to work in another city for a year versus working an extra hour at the office tonight. Such decisions may have equally important long-term effects. One study showed that the most successful professionals, those with the highest-paying jobs and the greatest recognition from their peers, also tended to have the most instances of divorce and estrangement from their children.[11] Naturally, none of these highly successful individuals consciously sacrificed their families for career advancement. Instead, they made hundreds of small trade-offs over time, such as staying late at the office instead of attending a child's school concert. The accumulation of these small choices gradually tipped their lives in one direction.

Indeed, we often underestimate the importance of the decisions we make each day. Rarely do we recognize that each of these choices presents an opportunity to learn, practice, and improve. Given this reality, we need a systematic method for integrating wisdom into our lives that is both simple and flexible — simple in that each step of the process follows a natural, easy-to-recall progression, yet flexible enough to apply the process to any question, problem, or dilemma.

The Seven Steps to Better Decision-Making

Consider your experience. On any given day, you might read an article, watch a presentation, or converse with a good friend. All these events are filled with wisdom. It follows, then, that this same wisdom now inspires you. However, those sparks often fade. For example, imagine reading an article about negotiating skills. You find it well-reasoned and valuable, as you plan to ask your boss for a salary increase in the next few months. You save it, intending to revisit it soon. However, a week later, you have forgotten it. When you finally meet with your boss, you revert to your usual patterns, struggle to advocate for yourself, and do not get the raise you wanted. Having all the wisdom in the world is useless unless you know how to access it when it counts.

We need a practical solution to address the challenge of retaining and applying wisdom. Such a process exists, comprising seven steps, a sequence anyone can master. The steps are as follows:

1. Ask the question.
2. Acknowledge your immediate response.
3. Seek perspective.
4. Envision someone wise.
5. Engage the voice of wisdom.
6. Act.
7. Observe and adapt.

The first four steps are investigative and create the conditions for engaging this voice of wisdom. The fifth step involves engaging the voice of wisdom, while the sixth calls for the courage to act once the correct choice is clear. The seventh step reminds us to reflect on that decision, learning from the results and, more broadly, all choices — ours and others'.

Adopting this process is akin to making a solemn promise or taking a vow. Here, you might imagine the word *vow* as an acronym for the *voice of wisdom*, emphasizing the commitment to seeking inner guidance. This vow entails recognizing that you have the power to choose at any moment. Part of that choice is whether to pause and summon the voice of wisdom to guide you toward the best decision.

But why make such a commitment? Because as humans, we not only have the power to choose, but we also possess the ability to anticipate the consequences of our choices. We are, in essence, moral agents responsible for our thoughts, words, and actions, even if we cannot fully escape the circumstances surrounding them. They remain our choices. This is both a gift and a responsibility of being human. A dog, even one as intelligent as a border collie, never wakes up and thinks, *I want to be a giraffe*, nor can it envision how such a choice might influence the future. We humans, on the other hand, are self-aware and capable of contemplating the far-reaching consequences of our actions. This capacity underscores the importance of continuously asking ourselves, *What is true?* in the present moment and *What is right?* as we weigh our choices for the future.

Summary

Chapter 1, "Why Wisdom?" establishes wisdom as the ability to recognize what is true, determine what is right, and to choose accordingly. Wisdom is not reserved for age, intellect, or experience alone. It is a practical skill that can be learned and applied to everyday decisions as well as defining moments. The seven steps introduced here provide a repeatable method for reconnecting with the voice of wisdom and making thoughtful, effective decisions. As you reflect on this chapter, consider the following questions:

1. When you think of wisdom, what qualities come to mind?

2. Across a typical day, how many of your choices arise from conscious deliberation rather than habit or impulse?

3. Which of the seven steps already influence how you make decisions?

4. How does wisdom appear in your decisions: as a feeling, a felt sense, an immediate knowing, or something else?

5. As you practice the seven steps, how might your approach to decision-making change?

Challenges

Self-Discovery: Set aside ten uninterrupted minutes to write about a decision in which you sensed clarity about what mattered most. Describe the situation and what helped you recognize what was true and what felt right. How did that understanding influence your choice? What did this experience reveal about how wisdom tends to appear in your own life?

Further Exploration: Have a conversation with someone you consider wise and ask them to reflect on how they approach important decisions. How do they discern what is true in a given situation? How do they decide what is right? What role does experience, reflection, or principle play in their choices? Afterward, consider which aspects of their approach you recognize in yourself and which you might want to develop further.

Chapter 2 — Why Now?

*Do not wait; the time will never be "just right." Start where you stand,
and work with whatever tools you may have at your command, and
better tools will be found as you go along.*
—Napoleon Hill[12]

Perhaps you accept the premise that wisdom enhances decision-making. You may even recognize the merit of a deliberate and structured process, such as the seven steps, in making significant choices. Yet a simple truth remains: Honing any skill requires dedication. Time and energy are finite, and countless pursuits compete for both, many offering more immediate gratification.

Why, then, should one pursue wisdom now? Why not wait until faced with a pivotal decision?

The answer lies in the interconnected nature of our environment. Decisions rarely exist in isolation. Their effects can extend outward, influencing relationships, communities, and circumstances beyond our immediate notice. Each choice carries the potential to alter not only our experience but also those around us.

This is why practice matters — today and every day. Wisdom is not confined to moments of great consequence; it informs the quieter, persistent choices that collectively define a life. Through forming deliberate habits, we prepare to meet the ordinary and extraordinary with understanding and intention.

It was this realization that first inspired me to write a book. Yet I repeatedly deferred the task. Writing, for me, is a slow art, akin to chiseling words, one by one, from unyielding stone. The conflict between living fully and setting aside the time to write weighed on me. Should I remain immersed in life or retreat to my desk to pour words onto a page? Then, one day, a startling news story caught my attention, dissolving my hesitation and solidifying my resolve to begin this work. The headline announced that we are rapidly approaching a point where the weight of plastic in our oceans will exceed the weight of all fish.[13]

The news was more than just alarming; it pointed toward something more disturbing. How many other stories on the multitude of pressing issues — social, political, economic, environmental — had I simply ignored or skimmed past? All the while, I continued with my life as if these problems existed in a parallel universe, one where I had little control or was somehow spared the consequences. Reading that headline, however, was different. I found myself asking not only *What does this mean for our planet?* but also *What does it reveal about our collective moral judgment?*

Whether due to timing, a sense of complicity, or a personal connection to the subject, I was forced to confront the widening dissonance between awareness and inaction. Not long before, I had sailed across the Pacific Ocean, witnessing firsthand the wonder and mystery of the sea while living off its bounty. During that same crossing, I encountered one of the vast garbage patches, a swirling vortex of human waste.

The experience left an indelible impression. What once seemed a far-off consequence of unchecked consumption had been made real. A vast, spreading ruination stained the world before my eyes. It was impossible to unsee. And once seen, it demanded answers.

Even if environmental issues are not your primary concern, sooner or later, you connect the dots and begin to wonder: *How will this affect the quality of our water? The availability of food?* What risks does this pose to the health and well-being of those I care about? And then it clicks: These problems are not just out there. They are here, woven into our daily lives. Once recognized, it cannot be ignored. The scale of the problem presses in, bringing with it a sense of urgency, a feeling that refuses to be ignored.

A reasonable response is outrage or anger, the kind that motivates action. Then, as the enormity of the challenges became clear, familiar questions arose, the same ones that often divert great achievements: *How can any one person make a difference? How can I make a difference?*

The answer is straightforward: You can. I can. And we must.

Where It Begins

Although we are products of our environment, our influence reverberates throughout it. This truth is verified by experience. Our lives result from countless decisions made by those before us and those around us, including our parents, peers, educators, and leaders. Simultaneously, advancements in science, technology, and communication have endowed us with unprecedented freedoms, corresponding responsibilities, and inherent risks. Moreover, as the challenges we face evolve in scale from local to regional to national to planetary, we can hardly ignore the persistent threats to our existence.

When confronting such issues, individually or as a species, it may be tempting to assign blame to a single person or group: *them, not us.* However, this oversimplification rarely reflects reality. The destruction of our oceans is the cumulative product of countless choices made over time. We may first look to corporations, governments, or industries, imagining them as faceless entities operating beyond our influence. But institutions are not monoliths; they are made up of people, each making decisions that accumulate over time. And at the origin of every decision, good or bad, is an individual or a specific group of individuals.

The accumulating waste in our oceans evinces this: how a single act of individual choice can set larger forces in motion. Somewhere, someone discarded the first bag of trash into the sea. Their identity and reasoning may remain forever unknown, but perhaps they rationalized it: *What harm could one bag of waste do in such a vast ocean?* That individual action did not occur in isolation. It contributed to a pattern, setting precedents, both good and bad, that others repeated. After that first transgression, someone else disposed of their waste in the ocean. Then, another person followed. And another. And another. Until one day, the practice became normalized and garbage fills the sea.

This is how it begins. And this is how it will end: one person at a time, taking a stand. Even if mounting dissatisfaction compels you to challenge the status quo, you quickly encounter the enormity of the problem. You may feel discouraged, tempted to give up or turn away. The urge is always there, to become lost in routine or the ever-present distractions that surround us. Or to fall into the trap of wishful thinking, expecting some revolutionary technology will remediate the damage. Yet the solutions to many large-scale problems can be as straightforward as their causes. This may require thinking in new ways and changing our habits: finding alternative materials, reusing, and recycling. It starts with one person, in one moment, deliberately pausing to consider their actions and then making the right choice. As one person adopts these practices, another follows. And another. Until one day, the process reverses, and no one throws garbage into the sea.

But no one must begin as someone. So why not you? Why not me?

Of course, this principle extends beyond the oceans. The ocean is merely a metaphor for our lives as a whole.

If I learn to make good decisions, my life improves. My relationships become stronger. I avoid mistakes that would cost me time, energy, or peace of mind. And if you learn to make good decisions, the same will be true for you. As we continue making these choices, others will inevitably do the same. Not only will our lives improve, but together we will begin to address the larger issues that once seemed beyond our reach. And one day, we will no longer ask, What can I alone do? Instead, we will say, Look what we have accomplished together.

The Expanding Weight of Responsibility

Whatever your span of influence today, one thing is certain: If you are caring or skillful, responsibility will find you. Over time, you will inevitably be drawn, or thrust, into roles that require good judgment.

Your work, whether done alone or as part of a large organization, provides a natural forum for practice. Managing a project, leading a team, or making strategic decisions requires the ability to weigh choices carefully. The best leaders grasp this intuitively. While gathering information is vital, they understand that effective decision-making transcends data analysis or rigid adherence to conventional practices. Instead, they take a broader approach: posing meaningful questions, considering multiple perspectives, and even seeking out opposing views, aware that no single person holds all the answers. Most importantly, they are willing to learn from mistakes and refine their process over time.

Yet work is only one domain in which judgment is tested. The same thoughtfulness you apply to professional decisions serves you well in every other part of life.

Here is where both experience and wisdom align: Life inevitably becomes more complex. As you move through different stages, the weight of your decisions increases. The responsibilities you take on, some by choice, others by necessity, will demand considered judgment and thoughtful action. Tending to your health, meeting the needs of a family, managing increasing work demands, caring for aging parents, and, eventually, confronting your mortality, all require discernment, patience, and resolve. Some decisions will be immediate and obvious; others will reveal their true significance only in time. Some of your decisions will directly affect the well-being of those closest to you; others will reach beyond your immediate view, influencing lives in ways you may only dimly perceive.

Consider the role of a caregiver entrusted with the well-being of another: a child, an aging parent, or even a beloved pet. Imagine facing a critical decision when medical advice seems uncertain or incomplete. As a caregiver, you might choose to seek a second opinion, weighing the inconvenience or cost against the possibility of better treatment. That single choice could significantly alter the outcome, whether it means uncovering a more accurate diagnosis or identifying a more effective solution. Such decisions reflect the immense responsibility inherent in caring for others, where even small actions can leave lasting effects on those who depend on you.

But responsibility is not limited to caregiving. The same discernment applies across all aspects of life — accompanying a friend through uncertainty, mentoring others, or making decisions that affect those around you. Time and again, you face a choice: wager on impulse or pause to weigh your options, increasing the probability of success.

In the end, decision-making is not just a skill but a discipline, one that grows sharper with practice. Yet wisdom is meaningless without action. What we choose, individually and collectively, determines not only the future but the world we leave behind.

What Is True? What Is Right?

While one might wonder whether the first person to throw a bag of garbage into the ocean knew the implications of their actions, we do. If we, as individuals or collectively, choose to stand by and do nothing today, what does this say about our future? Can we sincerely claim that we care for anyone or anything beyond ourselves?

Our awareness of the consequences demands action, starting with a reexamination of our thinking. We must recognize that *every choice matters*, not because we are all-powerful but because the power we have lies in our agency. Otherwise, we risk not only failing to resolve our current challenges but also creating new ones. How you begin your day, what you say to those around you, and the attitude you bring to work, each holds significance. Thus, the importance of taking a moment to pause, reflect, and allow wisdom to guide you.

If this seems like a significant time commitment or a daunting challenge, it need not be. Start by simply giving extra consideration to one choice. Pause for a moment. Engage the voice of wisdom within. Ask yourself: *What is true? And what is right?* Then, leave space for the answer. Do this today, and it will be easier to do the same tomorrow and again the day after that. In time, this practice will become a habit, and the habit will become an integral part of each day that follows.

While no process guarantees instant transformation, as you follow these steps, your choices will improve. Each good decision increases the likelihood that the next will be even better. This is not to suggest you will always get it right. None of us do. Nor does every decision turn out as intended. However, by applying the principles and practices outlined in this book, you can nurture a relationship with wisdom that will serve you well whatever the focus of your attention, from personal issues of the day to addressing global challenges. This aim is not to avoid guilt, wisdom has no regard for guilt, but to pursue the rewards it offers: clarity in uncertainty, steadiness in challenge, and the quiet confidence that each step you take advances you one step closer to the goals you seek and to a better life.

Ultimately, applying wisdom extends to every facet of our lives. Regardless of the circumstance or context, becoming a master decision-maker begins with learning to systematically and consistently make good decisions for ourselves. When we make choices guided by wisdom, we illuminate the lives around us. We become a force for progress, contributing to a brighter future for ourselves and generations to come.

And it all begins with a simple question: What is the wisest choice in this moment? Let us begin — one decision at a time. Will you continue?

Summary

Chapter 2, "Why Now?" argues that waiting for a perfect moment to act is itself a decision, often one that exacts hidden costs. Our choices do not occur in isolation. Each one contributes to patterns that affect our lives, our relationships, and the wider world. Because responsibility expands with influence and time, practicing wise decision-making cannot be postponed until a defining crisis arrives. By attending to everyday choices now, we prepare ourselves to respond with discernment and resolve when it matters most. As you reflect on this chapter, consider the following questions:

1. What is at least one example of a societal challenge that troubles you?

2. Have you ever felt tension between confronting this challenge and your perceived ability to effect change?

3. Can you recall a moment when a well-considered choice positively influenced your life?

4. In what ways did that decision benefit those around you, directly or indirectly?

5. What area of your life would benefit from more deliberate decision-making, and what makes this area stand out now?

Challenges

Self-Discovery: Spend ten minutes writing about a decision you have been postponing. Name what you are waiting for: more certainty, better timing, or additional information. Then note what has already been lost or constrained as a result of waiting. What remains unresolved, narrowed, or deferred because no choice was made?

Further Exploration: Choose one concern that weighs on you, personal or broader in scope, and discuss it with someone you trust. Rather than debating outcomes, focus on timing: What keeps people from acting sooner? What rationalizations make delay seem reasonable? As you reflect afterward, consider how those same patterns appear in your own decisions.

Chapter 3 — Ask the Question

Not everything that is faced can be changed,
but nothing can be changed until it is faced.
—James Baldwin[14]

When making any choice, the simplest and clearest place to begin is with a question. Questions focus your attention, prompt critical thinking, and may even challenge long-held beliefs. You need not have an answer. You need not possess all the information. What you need is something to hold on to.

Many choices come and go without notice. Others demand recognition. A question transforms vague worry into specific consideration. It offers a place to begin. It becomes a fingerhold, small but secure, when you find yourself pressed against a wall of uncertainty or doubt. It steadies the swirl of conflicting thoughts and fixes your attention on one discernible point. One grip. One reach. And with that, a way forward.

Questions can be formed across the full terrain of your life. Some bring order to the day, such as what comes first on the to-do list. Others reorder your life, such as choosing where you might live. Some are spoken aloud. Others remain unspoken. Whatever their form, questions refine vague unease into something sharper, more precise. They begin to reveal what is truly at stake.

Even acknowledging the question, silently to yourself or spoken aloud, can alter your relationship to the matter before you and, by extension, the options you perceive. The questions need not be large or dramatic. Often, the simplest ones lead to the most meaningful changes. Do I speak or wait? Do I step back or press forward? What matters more right now? These are not abstractions. They are handholds, each offering leverage when the rest of the wall appears too smooth to climb. To ask sincerely is to open oneself not only to answers but to change.

Without that grip, hesitation spreads. Concerns loop unanswered in the mind. Time passes. Options narrow. And when no question is brought to light, the world moves forward without you. Not because you lack resolve but because you failed to find something solid enough to hold.

Personal Account: Part One

For over a decade, I have worked in finance, specifically in private equity, which involves investing in and acquiring private companies. In addition to managing various aspects of the firm, I spend significant time evaluating prospective companies for investment, overseeing the acquisition process, and working closely with the leaders of acquired companies to help them increase profitability while positioning the business as the first choice to call on, whether as a prospective team member, partner, or provider.

I chose this work for several reasons. First, business is a powerful force, "the greatest system of social cooperation ever invented," as one thinker suggested.[15] It touches every aspect of our lives, providing a means of earning and delivering products and services while ideally offering an outlet for purpose or meaning. Second, finance, particularly private equity, allows me to work with intelligent and well-intentioned people who inspire me. Third, it requires continuous learning and improvement, especially in my role, given the diversity of industries in which we invest and the dynamic nature of business that demands ongoing evolution (and, in some cases, even revolution) to avoid stagnation and failure. Lastly, I value the opportunity to collaborate with company leaders, as their decisions can positively affect countless lives.

What most people I work with today may not know or no longer recall is that my career began in a different place. Before entering business, I practiced law for nearly fifteen years, focusing on business matters and commercial litigation. While I enjoyed aspects of being a lawyer, over time, I felt the legal field was not aligned with my desire to have more positive influence in people's lives; my approach to practicing law began troubling me.

Like many aspiring lawyers, I was drawn to the profession by the ideals of advancing just causes and helping those in need. In my early career, I never considered anything other than law. In a sense, the law fulfilled a personal myth, a self-image of being a noble warrior for the virtuous and oppressed. However, this vision was sustainable only for a limited period.

Over a decade, my partner, George, and I built a prosperous firm, achieving many traditional indicators of success. We represented notable clients, won hard-fought cases, and even set legal precedents. Our names appeared in the media, and affirmation followed, as did other rewards.

By our midthirties, we were each earning more than a million dollars a year, bringing financial security and the ability to acquire symbols of success. I recall strolling into a Porsche dealership, buying the latest 911 Carrera, a car I had never ridden in, and paying in cash. I purchased a platinum Rolex and gave away others as gifts. *Rewards for the initial risk, long hours, and success*, I reasoned. Yet the baubles I could afford were fleeting distractions from the discontent within. After a decade, the daily practice of law took a toll. People rarely call their lawyer on their best day. You will almost never hear "I just won the lottery!" or "We are having the best year ever!" Rather, people seek legal counsel when they encounter something they cannot resolve alone, whether it is advice on complex issues, escalating disputes, or the threat of a lawsuit. Years of rigorous training had sharpened my judgment and given me fluency in the complexities of business. I believed this expertise would allow me to stand as a trusted partner, someone to rely on in moments of uncertainty and need. Yet, as time passed, I began to feel more like a loyal watchdog peering through a picket fence: present, dependable, but granted only fleeting glimpses of the landscape. Summoned in times of trouble but never set free to run.

Few jobs are perfect. At some point, most people reflect on whether the career they are pursuing is the one they want to follow for the rest of their lives. I was no exception. In those moments, J. D. Salinger's words echoed in my mind: "How would you know you weren't being a phony? The trouble is, you wouldn't." I would reassure myself that once I achieved one more goal or won one more noble fight for justice, life would be easier and I could relax. Yet no level of success brought lasting contentment. Only after grasping the proverbial brass ring did I realize how cold it could be.

As time passed, a question arose: *Should I continue practicing law or pursue a new career in business?* The question demanded courage and thoughtful consideration. While the known role offered security and familiarity, the unknown alternative seemed to promise greater alignment with my values and priorities, and the chance to live that was truly my own.

The decision loomed, forcing me to confront whether I would abandon my dreams and everything I had built for a more fulfilling career. It was a defining moment, and my choice would determine the rest of my life.

To Be or Not to Be: Turning Issues into Answerable Questions

Consider an issue that has been troubling you. Dilemmas are a natural part of life; confronting them is essential for progress. Whether you are worried about your health, struggling with a work-related challenge, or unsure which school is best for your child, hold the issue in your mind and examine it closely. What is the specific problem? What small steps could help you begin to address this seemingly daunting challenge?

Without a well-defined question, any response may seem valid, but it is unlikely to provide clear direction. Concerns often manifest as vague statements or complaints, such as: *I do not want to become unhealthy like my father*, or *Michael is not doing his share at work*, or *Where should we send Caroline to school next year?* While these thoughts reflect genuine worries, they are not yet actionable questions.

To transform these concerns into questions that yield meaningful answers, frame them as closed-ended questions. A closed-ended question narrows your focus, forcing you to confront the central issue directly and bringing it into sharp relief. For example, instead of asking, *How would Caroline fare in private school?* ask, *Should we keep Caroline in public school or send her to private school next year?* This approach makes the decision more manageable, reducing the complexity to a binary choice.

Here is where you must resist the temptation to consider too many options or become absorbed in open-ended questions. There will be time later for more nuanced decisions, like exploring what programs a new school has to offer. Your goal now is to reduce the issue to a clear *A or B* choice. Too many options can lead to decision overload.[16] By framing the question in a way that invites a specific answer, you take the first bold step forward.

If simplifying the issue remains challenging, consider it through one of the classic categories of inquiry: who, what, why, when, where, or how. For instance, *Who will provide the best learning environment for Caroline?* addresses the who. *What are the benefits of public versus private school?* explores the what. *Why would private school be a better fit for her?* examines motivation. *When should we make this decision to ensure the best outcome?* looks at timing. *Where would Caroline thrive socially and academically?* addresses location. Finally, *How can we afford private school without compromising other priorities?* tackles the practical aspects.

By categorizing your concerns this way, you can better pinpoint the exact nature of your question. Once you have done so, simplify it further by reducing it to a *whether* or *which* question. For instance, after framing it as *What is the best schooling option for Caroline?* you can narrow it down to a binary choice: *Should Caroline stay in public school or transfer to private school?* This method of distilling the question keeps the decision-making process focused and manageable, preventing you from feeling overwhelmed and guiding you to clearer decisions.

At this stage, your goal is not to evaluate or solve the problem but to transform it into an answerable question. You do not need to scale the entire cliff at once, just find that first ledge.

As we often discover, seemingly opposite responses to an issue can illuminate a larger truth by revealing the complexity and duality inherent in many situations. Consider Shakespeare's "To be, or not to be" soliloquy (*Hamlet*, act 3, scene 1). Had he instead asked, "How can I ease the pain of losing my father?" he would have been inundated with advice like "Seek revenge," or "Let time pass," or "Talk to a friend." None of these responses addresses the core of his suffering. Hamlet cannot yet see beyond his grief. For him, the essence of the dilemma is far simpler: (A) to take his life in the hope of ending his pain or (B) to continue living despite the fear of greater suffering in the afterlife.

This stark choice, life or death, not only reflects Hamlet's internal struggle but also mirrors a broader human experience: the conflict we encounter when faced with the unknown. The unknown can be too vast for us to fathom. This is why breaking down an issue to its simplest questions, those that contemplate extremes, is so powerful, even if the situation itself is rarely black and white. We broaden our perspective and uncover deeper truths by earnestly contemplating such extremes.

When we explore these extremes, we often find that creative solutions emerge, ones that do not compromise either stance but combine their insights into a more comprehensive understanding. For Hamlet, the choice was not just between enduring suffering and choosing death. He found a middle way by pursuing justice by avenging his father's murder.

This same approach of confronting extremes can be applied when considering where to send Caroline to school. At first, the decision might seem to hinge on whether to keep her in public school or transfer her to a private institution. However, by asking the right questions, you can uncover broader possibilities. Perhaps there is a public school with a gifted program or smaller class sizes, or maybe a private school offers scholarships or sliding-scale tuition that makes it more accessible than initially thought. Just as Hamlet's existential dilemma crystallized into a course of action, your inquiry into Caroline's schooling can create new pathways beyond the initial choices.

Write It or Speak It to Set It Free

Sometimes we imagine that by focusing intensely on a problem, we can solve it simply by turning it over in our minds. This approach might work for objective questions, like *What is the best route between point A and point B?* or *What is the square root of 49?* — but it is less effective for the more subjective questions we frequently encounter. Consider the unexpressed question: *Should we vacation in Hawaii or visit relatives over the upcoming holiday?* Such unresolved questions can consume the mind, leaving open loops that drain your energy.

Once you have formed a question, the next step is to write it down or speak it aloud. To articulate the question is to release it and, in that act, to release yourself. In the mind, a question may remain a jumble of impressions and abstractions. Yet rendering it explicit requires the deliberate selection of language. That act of precision illuminates meaning and dispels ambiguity. As the words before you solidify, the burden and attachment you felt in the miasma of uncertainty begin to fade. Now, with dispassion and distance, the question may seem smaller, both in presence and emotional weight. What once felt overwhelming can now be approached with a sense of manageability. Suddenly, you not only have fingerholds on the cliff, but the cliff itself becomes measurable and manageable. By courageously voicing the question, you enter a realm where answering it is not only possible but inevitable.

Sharing the question with someone else is not necessary; what matters is making it real and specific. You could simply write it down or speak it aloud to yourself. Doing so objectifies it. You can study it, set it aside, or revisit it later.

Give it space.

The question exists for you; it is not you. It is an invitation to be the creator you are, to exercise your fundamental human power in the face of your circumstances. You have the power to choose your next step. Psychiatrist and author Viktor Frankl said, "Everything can be taken from a man but one thing: the last of the human freedoms — to choose one's attitude in any given set of circumstances, to choose one's own way."[17] Even if you cannot choose the circumstances, you can choose how to respond to them. The question you ask simply illuminates that the choice is, indeed, yours.

Now that you have made the first courageous move, take a moment to step back and appreciate the distance articulating the question has provided. Resist the urge to begin gathering evidence immediately. You might take a five-minute walk or a twenty-minute nap. You might go about the rest of your day and return hours or even days later. No matter how much distance you create, you can keep moving because you have captured and preserved the question — encoding it — and freeing it from your working memory.[18] It will be there when you are ready to pick it up again.

As the question becomes real and distinct from yourself, desires and answers begin to emerge. They might rise to the surface during your time away from the question or clearly present themselves on the page. Your closed question with possible responses (a or b) already offers potential solutions. As the answer begins to emerge within you, pay attention. There may be only two choices, or perhaps the creative part of you begins contemplating . . . Maybe there is a middle way?

Even a single breath can open up a universe of perspective. Sometimes, that is all it takes to begin.

Be Brave: Real Questions Require an Openness to Change

So what question has begun to awaken in you? Perhaps it is a sense that a part of your life can no longer continue unchanged. Some concerns arrive fully formed. *Do I want to be a parent? Can I manage my finances alone, or do I need help?* Others remain indistinct, still awaiting recognition. *Am I living in the place I wish to call home?* Naming either requires a measure of courage. Some require more. Once the question is made real, it cannot be made unreal. And once it has been spoken, even silently to yourself, it begins to demand a response.

Even the vaguest questions, when left unanswered, can give rise to a subtle sense of unease. If concern continues to linger, ask whether it is a passing discomfort or a true signal. Has it been ignored, postponed, managed into silence? If so, it likely deserves to be brought forward and named.

It is easy to defer hard questions. We postpone. We distract. We tell ourselves the timing is not yet right. Often, though, the real reason is simpler: Asking the question threatens what we know and what we have come to rely on. What once seemed solid, unshakable, reveals itself as merely habitual. The discomfort arises not because something might change but because we have finally allowed ourselves to see what already has.

Change, especially meaningful change, rarely begins in comfort. It asks something of us. It invites us to reconsider how we spend our time, how we relate to others, or how we live. Often, it requires that we relinquish what we know before reaching for something better. Yet even when the familiar no longer serves us, instinct urges resistance. We cling to what we believe we can control, confusing security for certainty and certainty for safety. But safety, in this form, is often a golden trap.

To break free of that resistance, begin by asking what has brought the question to the surface. Is it a restless desire for stimulation, change for its own sake, or is it a recognition that something foundational requires reexamination? There is a difference between boredom and the realization that the life you are living no longer reflects who you are.

If the question persists, if it emerges not from dissatisfaction but from something more enduring, then commit to follow it through. Let the question guide you. Let it test you. Let it draw from you the honesty you may not yet have spoken aloud.

While you may begin with two clear choices, allow yourself to remain open. The mind favors simplicity, especially in moments of distress: this or that, stay or go. But the value of the process is not in reaching a conclusion. It lies in what the inquiry itself reveals. What needs your attention? What has changed? What, exactly, is calling you forward now?

The most meaningful answers rarely reside at either end of a binary choice. They ask something more. You may begin by asking whether to continue down one course or take another, only to discover a third direction, one you had not considered, or a more fundamental question behind the one you first posed. What began as a decision may become an invitation to reconsider the structure altogether. This is not indecision. It is a creative thought arriving, often unannounced, asking you to look beyond what you may have envisioned before. Acknowledging this requires courage, the kind that brings what matters into view and holds it long enough to be named.

So what question continues to linger at the edge of your awareness just now?

Write it down. Speak it aloud. Make it real. Every honest question is a threshold. And every threshold marks a boundary. Passing through that boundary often leads somewhere worth exploring.

Summary

Chapter 3, "Ask the Question," explores the foundational step of articulating the question. A well-formed question transforms vague unease into something workable by fixing attention on what is truly at stake. It may arise from everyday concerns to life-altering choices. To ask honestly often brings unspoken fears or uncertainty to light. But it is through this vulnerability that we take the first step toward resolution. As you reflect on this chapter, consider the following questions:

1. What is a question you have avoided naming, and what has kept it unspoken?

2. What changes when a question moves from thought to words, whether written or spoken aloud?

3. When reduced to a clear either-or choice, what does your question reveal about the issue at hand?

4. Beyond the most obvious answers, what other possibilities might appear once the question is stated plainly?

5. What do you gain by addressing this question directly rather than allowing it to remain unresolved?

Challenges

Self-Discovery: Set aside fifteen minutes to list the concerns currently occupying your attention. Review the list and note which ones you have left vague or unspoken. Choose one and restate it as a clear, answerable question. Then pause and reflect: What became more defined once the concern took the form of a question?

Further Exploration: Share a current dilemma with someone you trust, without asking for advice. State the question aloud and listen to how it sounds when spoken. Notice whether new distinctions emerge or whether the question itself shifts. Does your friend respond with observations or questions that alter how you see the issue? Afterward, reflect on how articulating the question changed your relationship to it.

Chapter 4 — Acknowledge Your Immediate Response

Let the first impulse pass. Wait for the second.
—Baltasar Gracián

Let us begin this chapter with a short quiz focusing on your individual preferences. There are no right or wrong answers. Just notice what first pops into your mind as you read (or hear) each question:

1. When learning something new, do you prefer (A) starting with written instructions or (B) experimenting to figure things out along the way?

2. In your work setting, do you gravitate toward (A) tasks that keep you at a desk or (B) roles that involve being on the move?

3. For exercise, are you more likely to (A) attend a class at a gym or (B) enjoy the freedom of running or walking outdoors?

4. At social events, do you (A) feel energized by lively conversations in a crowd or (B) prefer smaller gatherings that encourage intimate discussions?

5. When reading, do you reach for (A) the tactile experience of a physical book or (B) the convenience of reading on a screen?

6. When selecting a movie or show, are you more likely to choose (A) a thought-provoking period drama or (B) an action-packed thriller?

7. For a weekend getaway, would you prefer (A) camping under the stars or (B) being pampered in a luxury hotel?

One or more of these questions likely prompted a clear response. Even if you are a cautious person who considers context, perhaps thinking, *It depends*, before responding, that reaction itself is telling. Although we as humans naturally experience strong desires and impulses, resist the urge to act on them immediately. Both science and literature agree that those initial impressions may not always reveal the whole truth.[19]

So what value do these initial impressions hold?

Effective decision-making requires balancing spontaneity with self-control, careful thought with quick action, and intuition with logic. Your unfiltered response is like a flash of lightning — briefly illuminating your desires or aversions in the landscape of your mind. Whether it reveals a path forward or warns of an approaching storm, these impulses offer insight into the mental processes behind your immediate awareness: the unconscious and subconscious mechanisms that distort your perceptions, emotions, and behaviors. Examining these responses may uncover the true motivations, inhibitions, and influences guiding your decisions.

Consider, for example, what a preference between physical and digital books might reveal. A fondness for physical books may arise from the satisfaction of touching paper, indicating a preference for tangible experiences. It might also reflect a desire for simplicity in an increasingly digital world. Conversely, favoring digital books may stem from a focus on practicality and an appreciation for convenience and portability. This preference might also indicate an innate adaptability and openness to technological advancements.

Like leaves on a tree, our responses are swayed by the wind of our emotions, the water of our experiences, and the soil of our beliefs. The most important task is to observe these elements objectively, much like a scientist studying changes in a forest ecosystem. As you engage in this process, be patient with yourself. Contradictions may emerge, and that is entirely natural. Each response develops in its way, ideally reaching toward the light.

Personal Account: Part Two

For anyone who has invested years into a pursuit, whether a career, relationship, or personal goal, the prospect of change can evoke both dread and tantalizing possibility. This sentiment rings especially true for lawyers. Given the time and resources the legal profession demands, the aspiration to change careers often lingers as an enticing daydream. However, when I finally asked myself, *Should I remain in law or pursue a career in business?* an answer immediately surfaced in my mind: *I want out.*

This realization was surprising yet unsettling, like a long-ignored message finally acknowledged. Reflecting on the years of lost sleep and frequent stomachaches, my passion for law had faded. Mondays filled me with dread, while the prospect of a future in business brought both apprehension and exhilaration. The potential for building mission-driven enterprises intrigued me, but I had to consider the risks: career setbacks, financial instability, uncertain success, and necessary sacrifices.

If I pursued business and failed, would my years and resources in law be wasted? More importantly, was I equipped to succeed? My experience managing a law firm and advising business owners suggested I had the capacity. But how much did I truly know about the broader landscape of business?

Once the surprise subsided, I returned to familiar territory: analysis and reasoning. Armed with a lawyer's analytical skills, I prepared to examine the case for change.

The Case for Business

One rewarding period of my legal career was when I stepped away from daily practice to serve as the chief executive officer of a group of senior-care facilities. This role thrust me into business operations and human services. The parent company was in financial distress, and a court appointed me to take charge. My duty was to manage the assets for the creditors' benefit. However, my first visit to a facility revealed it was to be far more than a business. It was a community of fragile lives.

The residents' care required a delicate balance between autonomy and attentive support. In our first meeting, the director of operations stressed the importance of relationships, as well as the meals and social activities that revolved around them. Then, she said with a conspiratorial tone, "There is something you need to understand from the outset."

"Okay," I replied, wondering where the conversation was going.

She continued, her voice direct, "The residents here are quite active, and I mean *sexually* active."

I blinked, processing this unexpected information.

After a moment, she straightened up and asked, "Shall we head to the cafeteria for lunch?"

Beyond the residents, several groups relied on the business. Employees depended on ongoing employment, suppliers needed assurance of payment, and the surrounding community needed a caring home for the people they loved. The decisions the other managers and I would make affected all these groups and more.

Together, as a team, we revitalized the business by addressing the needs of all involved. We improved care, enhanced employee benefits, and settled outstanding vendor payments. We upgraded the kitchen, laundry, and common areas to create a more welcoming environment. We purchased new vans for transporting residents to appointments and social activities. These efforts led to the highest state rating for care and transformed the business from a money-losing operation to one generating surplus income for investment.

During my time managing the facilities, I worried about receiving calls about resident injuries, medication errors, or residents wandering away. Yet this experience sparked a desire to contribute more broadly to people's lives. It highlighted how my skills as a lawyer — critical thinking, communication, accountability, and adaptability — could be valuable in business. Moreover, the role provided unexpected professional development in finance, human resources, marketing, and team dynamics, opening my eyes to how I could meaningfully contribute in a life beyond the law.

The Case for Staying in Law

While fulfilling, my brief immersion in business prompted me to evaluate my career in a new way. Although potentially less gratifying, the legal field offered a clearer, more straightforward track. Perhaps switching careers was too extreme? I considered options within the legal profession: starting a firm aligned with my ideals, joining a more prominent firm, or working in-house for a company. I even contemplated seeking public office, though campaigning held little appeal. However, none of these alternatives matched the excitement and purpose I found in business.

The fear of failure loomed large, with high stakes and risk of career regression. I had seen colleagues attempt transitions with mixed results: One became a forest ranger, only to find he was allergic to trees; another turned high-stakes poker player, winning big before going broke; and a third became a fighter pilot, never looking back. The need to return to legal practice, as I observed among those who failed, was a genuine concern. Still, questioning my career felt liberating. I trusted that through self-reflection and diligence, I would find the right direction, whether staying in law or pursuing something new, always with awareness and intention.

Notice What Arises, Free of Judgment

The mind is a formidable tool, drawing on knowledge, experience, and reasoning to contend with life's complexities. When confronted with a question, it quickly generates an initial response — whether a word, sensation, thought, desire, or apprehension. This spontaneous reaction holds valuable information, though acting on it impulsively is not always wise. Allow these impressions to surface in your awareness without judgment. While these first impressions often take the form of a single word or phrase, they may hold layers of meaning that belie their simplicity.

When a spontaneous reaction surfaces, you are not merely encountering a fleeting thought — you are glimpsing a reflection of your innermost self. These reactions reveal not just preferences but the very foundations of your identity, formed by the interplay of experience, ideals, and subconscious beliefs.

For instance, when asked, *Where would you like to go on your next vacation?* your mind might immediately answer, *Hawaii*. Yet *Hawaii* is not merely a destination; it serves as a proxy for a host of associations: serene beaches, gentle waves, tropical warmth, vibrant landscapes, volcanic adventures, or the allure of escape and relaxation.

This instant creation of vivid imagery demonstrates how our minds process decisions and experiences. Whether the response is *Hawaii*, a simple *The beach*, or even *Not that*, take note of recurring thoughts and physical sensations and carefully consider the narrative they suggest. There is always more beneath the surface of your conscious thoughts, waiting to be explored.

However, the mind is not infallible. Its inclination toward order, pattern, and design, the metaphysical mantra of modernity, can lead it astray, filling gaps with biases or resisting change. To counter this, pay attention to your thoughts, as well as the signals from your body and heart. Each offers unique insights that complement the mind's deliberations.

The body, anchored in the present, often perceives subtle cues before the mind fully processes them. We have all experienced this: A family member or boss enters a room, and your body tenses even before you hear the words "We need to talk." Your stomach may tighten, signaling anxiety or fear of change. Alternatively, depending on the tone or words used, you might feel a lightness in your muscles, indicating alignment with the possibilities ahead. These physical reactions can provide critical clues, often bypassing the mind's filters.

Similarly, the heart, the wellspring of emotion and connections, offers a distinct perspective. It allows you to perceive your environment through the lens of relationships and shared experiences. It reminds us that our lives are intrinsically linked to those around us, from close loved ones to distant strangers we will never meet. When your heart senses these bonds, whether through shared lineage or common experience, you may feel a surge of empathy or understanding, signaling a desire for closeness or unity.

Recognize these responses for what they are: messengers conveying insights about your desires, fears, preferences, and beliefs. Notice any tensions and contradictions: Perhaps your mind advises caution while your heart urges further exploration. Instead of seeking a resolution, allow these signals to coexist, each contributing its truth. The mind's instinct for preservation and the heart's invitation to discovery are not adversaries but complementary forces. By honoring both, you may discover a middle way that balances caution with courage.

Whatever arises, remain open and curious. Trust your intuition to guide you where logic alone may falter. By attending to spontaneous reactions and exploring their subtleties, you may uncover unexamined truths: about yourself and the question itself.

Acknowledge Your Immediate Response

Once your initial impression arises, capture it. This is where your humanity truly shines.

Use the tools at your disposal, whether a pencil or keyboard, to record your abstract thoughts and feelings. This seemingly simple exercise bridges the ephemeral realm of thought with the solidity of words, giving form to your inner world. As you do this, allow your response to exist without judgment or censorship. Do not filter your thoughts; instead, let them flow freely, welcoming all emotions, instincts, and desires that emerge. Your initial impulse is neither right nor wrong, nor does it define you entirely. It merely reflects this moment, under these specific circumstances — a point-in-time rendering of your present state. If asked the same question at another time, you might have a different answer. As you evolve, so, too, will your responses.

By capturing your initial thoughts and feelings, you engage in a process that transcends mere reflection. This acknowledgment serves as a vital step in understanding the unseen currents that influence your decisions and actions.

Articulating these thoughts, whether spoken aloud or written down, transforms your relationship with them. It creates a subject-object dynamic, creating the distance needed to evaluate your response more impartially. This process serves as a foundation for inquiry, analysis, and self-evaluation. The act itself holds intrinsic value even if you never revisit what you have written. But do.

Make a List and Check It Twice
Now, having acknowledged this initial impulse, this incipient curiosity, picture yourself standing at a crossroads, facing a decision that could significantly alter the course of your life. How would you proceed?

Start by listing the reasons for and against acting on your initial impulse. This exercise disrupts reflexive reactions, safeguards against rushed decisions, and promotes more deliberate self-reflection. It minimizes the emotional bias and impulsive behavior that often leads to errors and regret.

Imagine considering a career change. As you outline the reasons for and against it, you might find that the excitement of new challenges outweighs the comfort of your current role, prompting you to explore possibilities you had not previously entertained.

Even seemingly simple decisions can involve a complex array of interrelated factors. For instance, choosing between two job offers might involve considerations such as salary, personal time, opportunities for professional development, the work environment, or relocating to a more appealing city. Externalizing these factors into a list compels you to simplify and clarify your reasoning, as though explaining the matter to someone unfamiliar with the situation. This process helps you see the central issues more clearly and prompts important questions: *Are these assumptions factual? How confident are you in these responses?*

This exercise invites you to consider a broad spectrum of possible outcomes, including those you might overlook. Ask yourself: *What are the implications if my initial judgment proves mistaken?* Creating distance between yourself and the decision allows for a clearer, more measured evaluation of its merits.

This time-honored method of self-evaluation has a rich and enduring history. Respected figures, including Ben Franklin and Charles Darwin, employed this technique. Franklin viewed lists as a form of moral algebra for uncovering truth,[20] while Darwin applied it to his decision about whether to marry.[21] Darwin's use of this method for such a personal choice highlights how rational analysis can complement emotional considerations in life-changing decisions. However, it is important to note that this process, with its emphasis on logical analysis, also has its limits. Even Sigmund Freud, a pioneer in the analytical study of the mind, recognized the vital role of intuition in major life choices. He noted, "When making a decision of minor importance, I have always found it advantageous to consider all the pros and cons. In vital matters, however, such as the choice of a mate or a profession, the decision should come from the unconscious, from somewhere within ourselves."[22]

Indeed, in the steps ahead, we will explore the interplay between analytical reasoning and intuition, learning to harness both for more effective decision-making. At this juncture, however, our focus is on articulating the thoughts swirling in your mind and then weighing them. Lists may not always yield definitive answers, but the ability to entertain opposing viewpoints while contemplating a response is a hallmark of prudent decision-making.[23] This process often reveals hidden truths, sparks novel solutions, or uncovers paradoxes worthy of further examination. Externalizing your thoughts enhances objectivity, turning abstract concerns into tangible ideas and making even the most daunting decisions more manageable and approachable.

So what does the process look like?

While mental reflection has its place, visually arranging your thoughts offers unique benefits. As you commit ideas to paper or screen, abstract notions crystallize into concrete form. Patterns emerge. Connections reveal themselves. And solutions you had not considered may suddenly become apparent. Most important, seeing your ideas laid out before you might prompt a reconsideration of perspective. You may find yourself stepping back to ask larger questions: *How significant is this decision in the grand scheme of things? Is this the real issue I should be focusing on?* In this way, the simple act of externalizing your thoughts can lead to unexpected insights and more purposeful decision-making.

Wondering if this is true? Take a moment to consider a question that has been on your mind. Or imagine how you might apply this process to everyday dilemmas that many of us encounter. For example, whether to:

pursue a degree

start a new job

change careers

launch a new business

begin a relationship

end a relationship

get married

buy a home

have a child

care for a family member.

Whether it is your question or one you have chosen for practice, begin by cataloging as many arguments as possible, both for and against each choice. Think freely and widely. Jot down whatever comes to mind. At this stage, aim for quantity over quality. You will have the opportunity to edit later. Allowing your mind to roam freely reveals previously unconsidered aspects of the decision. For instance, if considering a career change, you might list *increased job satisfaction* and *opportunity to learn new skills* as pros and *loss of seniority* and *temporary financial instability* as cons.

Next, incorporate objective information relevant to your decision. This step grounds your choices in reality rather than speculation. Consider consulting multiple sources to ensure a well-rounded view. For a career change, include data from compensation surveys, industry publications, and government labor statistics. You might also review hiring trends, conduct interviews with experts, or examine reports about companies you are considering.

While objective data is important, do not underestimate the significance of your emotional responses. These feelings often highlight misalignments with our intentions or raise concerns that are vital to our overall satisfaction with a decision. Consider factors such as time for your personal life, potential for advancement, and alignment with personal values. You might note *excitement about new challenges* or *sense of renewed purpose* as emotional pros. Conversely, *anxiety about leaving a familiar environment* or *fear of failure in a new role* could be emotional cons. Such insights can help illuminate your underlying motivations and concerns.

As you create your list, note any gaps in your knowledge. These gaps present opportunities for further research, enhancing the quality and reliability of your decision-making process. Acknowledging what you do not know is often as valuable as knowing what you do.

Later, you can dedicate time to exploring these areas to make a more informed decision.

Finally, review and evaluate your list to determine the most compelling arguments for each choice. At this stage in the process, aim to reduce your original list to no more than three to five points for and three to five points against. This may involve synthesizing several ideas into broader concepts. For instance, if you are contemplating a career change, you might group *higher salary*, *better benefits*, and *performance bonuses* under the single category of *improved financial prospects*.

Pay close attention to how your personal experiences, beliefs, and assumptions influence your views. Be wary of confirmation bias, where you unconsciously favor information that supports your preexisting beliefs. Consider not only your individual experiences but also broader societal expectations, cultural influences, and advice from trusted sources. These subtle yet powerful forces can significantly sway decisions.

To counter these influences, actively seek and fairly consider information and perspectives that challenge your initial inclinations. For example, conventional wisdom might suggest that the only way to career success is through long hours of work or that starting a business is purely glamorous. You may also feel pressure to appear productive or to curate the image of a flawless life. A practical way to uncover hidden biases is to reverse the situation. If you were advising a friend in the opposite situation, what would you say? This deliberate role reversal can reveal inconsistencies in your reasoning and help ensure a more balanced evaluation.

As you approach the end of the process, the scales should ideally tip in one direction or the other. However, if no clear preference emerges, ask yourself:

1. What is the central issue at stake?

2. What are the strongest arguments for and against each choice?

3. How do your past experiences and beliefs influence your perspective?

4. Which choice best aligns with your long-term aspirations?

Decision-making is often an iterative process that requires time and patience, especially for significant life choices. Feel free to revisit and refine your list. You might set it aside for a day or two as you gather more information and gain new perspectives. As you engage in routine tasks, your subconscious mind, now informed by the evidence, will continue to deliberate. When you return to the decision afresh, allow yourself the flexibility to adapt to new insights that have emerged. Though some uncertainty will always exist, these realizations can often provide the confidence to move forward.

A Shift in Perspective

Returning to the question I was grappling with — *Should I (A) continue practicing law or (B) or pursue a new career in business?* — an objective evaluation of my list, treating each item with equal weight, seemed to point toward remaining in law. Yet a splinter of discontent disrupted my peace. I sensed the tension in my body and a void in my heart. Remaining in law was not the right answer. Something larger was at stake, which I was only beginning to perceive after acknowledging this unfulfilled longing: Was a vision from the past still serving me today, or was I serving it? This inquiry — the question behind the question — probed the very center of my being, illustrating the transformative insights that emerge when we listen to our inner wisdom.

My life had been built on the identity of being a lawyer. The drive to succeed and the resulting achievements had, for years, diverted me from questioning this direction. However, my success exposed a significant fault line. I was steadily becoming exhausted, not from work itself but from the lack of fulfillment it provided. This realization did not necessarily mean a different career would be more rewarding — that consideration would become important later. In that moment, I perceived the loss of an ideal, or more accurately, the loss of belief in that ideal. I realized that my decade-long investment in this career might also be hindering my ability to see clearly. To make a true assessment, I needed to gain some distance for perspective.

Speaking the question aloud disentangled it from an intrinsic part of my identity to something I could objectively examine: a tension to manage or a problem to solve. In a literal sense, I could write it on a piece of paper and set it aside for further examination later. Yet, as soon as I voiced the question, a spark of excitement flickered within me. The possibility of a new career energized me, not just for the challenge it represented but also because I sensed it was the direction I should have pursued long ago. A fresh start would involve challenges, yet my legal skills could transform these obstacles into opportunities. By reframing my experience as preparatory rather than wasted, starting over seemed less daunting. The most profound realization was paradoxical: *To become the lawyer I aspired to be, I had to leave the practice of law behind.*

With an open perspective, each stage of life presents opportunities to acquire new capabilities that serve you in unexpected ways. Possibilities begin to outweigh obstacles, understanding emerges, and your choices become commitments fueled by purpose and conviction.

While acknowledging initial responses and evaluating pros and cons are necessary first steps, they are insufficient for true wisdom and may even prove counterproductive. Many stop at this juncture, confirming biases and constraining their potential. As economist Thomas Schelling noted, even rigorous analysis cannot reveal what we have never considered.[24] To make genuinely wise choices, we must seek broader perspectives, uncover hidden possibilities, and align decisions with our intentions and aspirations. This underscores the importance of the next step: seeking perspective. By broadening your view, you enrich your understanding and uncover options that might otherwise remain out of reach.

Summary

Chapter 4, "Acknowledge Your Immediate Response" focuses on what appears the instant a question is asked. That first reaction may arrive as a thought, a feeling, or a physical signal, and it often reflects habit or desire rather than considered judgment. By capturing it without judgment and placing it on the page, you create distance from it and can see it more clearly. Writing or listing what arises turns an impulse into something observable, making it possible to question assumptions and slow the urge to act. This step does not decide the matter. It reveals what is already influencing the choice before reflection begins. As you reflect on this chapter, consider the following questions:

1. Think of a recent significant decision. What was your immediate reaction?

2. What influences were present in that first reaction, including past experience, perceived expectations, or your emotional state?

3. When time allows, what changes when you pause before responding?

4. When you list reasons for and against an action, what does the exercise reveal?

5. How might such a list illuminate the assumptions, beliefs, or priorities that are influencing your response?

Challenges

Self-Discovery: Choose a past decision you still question. State the issue as you understood it at the time and note what you chose to do. Then write two brief lists: reasons that supported your choice, and reasons that pointed toward a different course. Reflect on what you were protecting, what you were seeking, and what this reveals about the forces influencing your initial response.

Further Exploration: For the next twenty-four hours, when someone asks you a question or seeks your advice, take one mindful breath before answering. Notice what rises first, whether a thought, a feeling, or an impulse and let it register without judgment. Take a second breath, then reply. At day's end, write a few lines on what you observed and whether that brief pause affected the content or quality of your replies.

Chapter 5 — Seek Perspective

It is the mark of an educated mind to be able
to entertain a thought without accepting it.
—Aristotle[25]

As humans, our remarkable ability to remember the past and envision the future sets us apart. However, when our thoughts focus solely on ourselves, we risk overlooking broader perspectives that could provide invaluable insights. This is where our innate compassion — what the Chinese philosopher Mencius called the "heart-mind which feels for others"[26] — becomes essential. Such compassion broadens our viewpoints, enriching our choices not only by considering others' perspectives but also by helping us view our circumstances with greater objectivity.

Having formulated your question and acknowledged your immediate response, it is time to pause and widen the aperture. This step invites a broadening of perspective, allowing you to transcend a narrow point of view and explore all aspects of your decision, a process akin to walking around a statue and observing it from every angle. As you expand your considerations, think about the following: Who else could be affected by this choice? The answer could include family, friends, colleagues, and numerous others who intersect with your life. Like you, all these people have their unique points of view, and their insights can prove invaluable if you share your questions with them.

Each new perspective has the potential to unveil persuasive arguments or important considerations that might not have occurred to you in solitude. Ignoring these perspectives risks making choices based on incomplete information. The ultimate goal is not just to make a decision but to make the right decision. By considering multiple perspectives, you gain a clearer understanding of your decision's full scope, its potential effects, and how it might influence the lives of both yourself and others, thus increasing the likelihood of making a wise and well-informed decision.

Personal Account: Part Three

A potential career change, like all significant decisions, carried substantial real-world implications. Contemplating the decision or listing reasons for and against it might seem like a simple exercise, but the reality is far more complex. Choosing to act, whether to maintain my current course or adopt a new one, could fundamentally recast my life and the lives of those around me. The interconnections between these choices and their potential effects underscored the need for a comprehensive understanding.

The decision required a thorough examination from diverse viewpoints, careful weighing of opportunities, and sincere consideration of potential challenges. Was this yearning for change a genuine calling or merely a reflexive response to recent events or fleeting discontent? Could I be idealizing the business environment, overlooking hidden complexities and risks? Pondering these questions went beyond mere validation; it was essential to ensure my decision would not lead to future regret.

How would I accomplish that? Who could help me see the matter from multiple viewpoints, including those challenging my assumptions? The answer was not just one individual but a diverse group of individuals, each offering their unique concerns and perspectives for a more complete understanding.

I began by listing everyone who could be affected, starting with those closest to me and extending to our wider professional circle. At the farthest boundaries, the list included supporting specialists such as consulting experts, court reporters, and couriers, whose businesses depended on the continued need for their services; the local bar association, which could lose a member's patronage; and potential new clients referred to our firm. For those seeking help in my focus areas, a departure from the law would likely pose a minor setback. Who could we entrust to continue this work for these groups?

Narrowing the focus, I concentrated on those most affected by my potential career change: my then-wife; my law partner, George; our staff, clients, and colleagues; and, to a lesser degree, my friends. My decision would directly influence my wife, as my salary contributed to our financial well-being. George would need to replace me or redistribute my responsibilities, leading to changes in our relationships with clients and staff. I needed to weigh the professional and emotional consequences of my decision. I wanted to avoid causing unnecessary concern about my commitment to the firm if, ultimately, I opted not to proceed.

With these factors in mind, I began by asking my wife. As a fellow lawyer, she understood the challenges of legal work, from looming deadlines to social hierarchies within the legal field. She well understood the ambiguous boundary between the pursuit of justice and financial reward. Beyond practical concerns like money and where I would work, she expressed emotional concerns, noting signs of my heightened stress, including longer hours, distraction, and withdrawal.

Even without voicing her worries directly, I sensed my wife's concern through subtle changes in her demeanor. Her response prompted me to reflect on the toll my career was taking on both my well-being and hers, thereby revealing the potential benefits of a change.

Next, I envisioned George's response. Brilliant but volatile, he was a formidable force in the courtroom yet often emotional. He relied on my rationality for balance in our relationship. We complemented each other: my sound to his fury. Given our shared history and assumed future, I anticipated he might disapprove or become angry at the prospect of my departure. Finding another partner or assuming the role of managing the firm would require time and a marked change in his behavior and responsibilities. I knew well enough that he would resist.

Gauging George's likely reaction required careful consideration of our partnership dynamics. I kept asking myself, *Can I trust his motives?* Would his advice come from genuine concern for our practice's success and our clients' well-being? Or would it be influenced by his personal needs, resistance to change, or rivalry?

What about our staff and clients? Their livelihoods were inextricably intertwined with our firm's daily operations. Change raised questions about their roles and relationships, and the firm's future. They would want stability and assurance that operations would continue without upheaval. Given their reliance on job security and career development, I needed to acknowledge their need for a clear succession plan.

Next came my professional circle, the lawyers I interacted with daily. In the fiercely competitive law profession, particularly trial law, trust is rare. The environment is rife with opportunism, and any hint of uncertainty could be exploited. Thus, discussing my thoughts with anyone but George posed a considerable risk. Only a few close friends could be confided in. Thankfully, those I approached understood my situation and its implications. Still, uncertainty lingered.

I also sought the viewpoints of friends in business, from seasoned executives to entrepreneurs. While they were less familiar with my situation, they acted as an informal advisory board, offering unbiased views unrelated to their financial stakes. A college friend in banking dispelled some business mystique, making the transition seem more attainable. Another friend, an entrepreneur, shared the challenges and exhilaration of building a business. A third friend, a physician in the midst of his career change, helped me explore the practicalities of change.

Each contributed valuable insights into the business community, highlighting both opportunities and risks. Some praised the decision, encouraging me with sentiments like, "Good for you for leaving." Others cautioned against hasty decisions, with one warning, "Be careful not to throw away years of hard work and success."

Still, a persistent question remained: Could I ever sever my connection with the law?

Even among close friends, I hesitated to discuss the expanding gap between my work and aspirations. I longed for meaningful engagement and wanted to feel that my work benefited a wider community. Most days, I felt like a chess player, making calculated moves against the clock. Winning a case with substantial financial rewards helped one client, yet I questioned whether transferring wealth from one affluent party to another truly contributed to the greater good. The relationships felt transactional, leading me to question my career and the legal profession.

Most people were never aware of the emotional strain work caused me. As most lawyers do, I maintained a facade of competence and composure in my professional life. Empathy is vital in the law; we must take on our clients' burdens, making their cases our own. However, the emotional weight of my work often went unnoticed. They did not see the fatigue and stress I took home on Fridays or the anxiety that crept in on Sunday nights (which I began to refer to as the Sunday night blues). They did not realize I had resorted to coping mechanisms like shopping or snacking for momentary escape. The relentless pursuit of happiness always seemed just out of reach. Each week, the internal struggle intensified. While exercise provided some relief, the voice inside my head grew louder, urging me to pursue a new way. Exiting the law might not resolve all my concerns, but it offered a tangible step away from a life marked by dissonance and dissatisfaction.

Changing careers was not merely a choice between law and business; it was a commitment to living authentically, aligning my decisions with aspirations I had yet to fully understand when I began in law. Would I succeed? Only the future would tell. However, the diverse perspectives gathered from those around me strengthened my resolve to move forward.

Everyone and Everything Is Connected

While we may value, even cherish, our sense of freedom or independence, the undeniable truth remains that our history, culture, and circumstances were largely established before our arrival. As German philosopher Martin Heidegger posited, we are "thrown into this world,"[27] beneficiaries of countless decisions, both noble and flawed, made by those who preceded us. This realization highlights the inextricable interconnectedness of our lives, a truth that extends beyond philosophical musings or the complex equations of quantum physics.

Consider your environment. The architecture of the buildings around you, the home you live in, the transportation you rely on, and the technology that connects us are all the result of the work of countless architects, engineers, and innovators. Beyond these societal contributions, think of the individuals whose choices have influenced your fate. Reflect on how your great-grandparents' decision to immigrate or remain in their homeland influenced your family history. Or how your parents' choices — to marry, to have a child, to live in a particular neighborhood — influenced the course of your life. Teachers, mentors, bosses, trendsetters, and policymakers have all forged our individual and collective preferences and expectations. Yet, despite these myriad influences, we alone retain agency over our thoughts, words, and actions.

Every decision, past and present, initiates a series of cause and effect, a concept often referred to as karma. Contrary to popular belief, karma does not represent a cosmic system for justice, rewarding good deeds and punishing bad ones. Instead, it merely points to the origin of events: an action sets a chain of occurrences in motion, ultimately leading to that result. This deceptively simple principle demonstrates the intrinsic link between our actions and their consequences, reminding us that, despite our best efforts to plan, the outcomes of our choices often emerge in ways we neither intend nor foresee.

Imagine each choice, yours and others, as a stone tossed into a pool of water. Some choices may seem insignificant, causing barely noticeable ripples. Others may encounter hidden currents, collide with opposing waves, or unleash a tsunami of monumental force. Thus, we must continually ask ourselves: Who will these waves reach? How will they alter the surface of the pool and the unseen depths below?

Recognizing such interconnectedness prepares us for the next critical step in decision-making: identifying who will be affected by our choices and thoughtfully considering their perspectives.

Who Will Be Affected, and What Might They Suggest?

As you approach your decision, identify the individuals, groups, and institutions that may be affected by your choice. These parties can vary widely depending on the nature of the issue before you. Each decision radiates outward, affecting lives in ways not always immediately visible. At this stage, think broadly and imaginatively. Aim to identify as many potentially affected parties as possible. (At least five is a good start.)

In personal matters, the affected may include not only immediate family but also extended relatives, close friends, neighbors, or trusted advisors such as a physician, therapist, or financial consultant. In professional settings, the circle may widen to encompass clients or customers, colleagues, employees, supervisors, vendors, legal or financial partners, and even civic institutions or professional associations. At times, the community in which your organization operates — its reputation, economy, or fabric of daily life — may also be influenced. As you consider each of these, do more than list them. Ask what your decision might demand of them. What new responsibilities could it introduce? What possibilities might it create?

Once you have your list, begin to refine it. To keep your thinking focused, prioritize those most directly affected — the individuals or groups who will feel the consequences first or most acutely. Then consider the degree and duration of those effects. Will they be minimal or substantial? Brief or enduring? For instance, the choice to launch a missile entails irreversible consequences and affects many. Choosing what to eat for lunch, by contrast, is a matter of personal preference. Your decision likely falls somewhere between these extremes. Ask yourself: What challenges might each person face as a result? What possibilities, welcome or not, might this choice set in motion?

With this awareness, return to each name on your list and ask yourself: What might this person suggest? Their priorities may differ from yours, but their perspective could surface something you have not yet considered, affirming your instincts or challenging them in meaningful ways. What are they likely to say, and what might that reveal about their concerns, hopes, or expectations?

When we weigh a difficult decision, it helps to consider how that decision may affect others, not only what they may say but what they may feel or silently carry.

For instance, if you are considering ending a long-term relationship, the first to feel its effects are likely to include your partner, your children (if you have any), and close family members. Your partner might express anger, regret, or a desire to work through your differences. He might suggest couples therapy or a trial separation, or raise concerns about shared finances or parenting responsibilities. Some proposals may reflect genuine care. Others may stem from fear: of being alone, of change, or of losing the life you have built together. Some may reflect an attachment to what is familiar or a need to protect the status quo.

Children, too, if involved, may worry about losing the sense of home they know. Their concerns might range from logistical ("Where will I live?") to emotional ("Will I see both of you?"). Even without articulating it, they may carry fears about how this change will affect their relationships and the rhythm of daily life. Consider not only what they might say aloud but what they may not know how to say.

Close family members may respond with unease, disappointment, or even relief. Some may offer practical support: help with the children, a temporary place to stay, or introductions to useful resources. Others may offer stories from their own lives, not as prescriptions but as expressions of solidarity. Their responses may contain wisdom but also personal bias, especially if your decision invites them to reconsider choices they once made but never fully examined.

As you take in these imagined or real perspectives, you may find yourself revisiting earlier decisions, not out of regret but to understand them more clearly. The aim is not to linger in the past but to see more plainly the forces that have brought you to this point, and to proceed with steadiness and care.

Consider Asking

If the nature of the question allows, or if the effects on another person are significant, consider going beyond merely adding his or her name to the list. Ask for their perspective directly. This might feel uncomfortable, particularly if their views differ from yours. That discomfort, however, is often a signal that their insight could prove valuable.

Inviting alternative perspectives offers a momentary retreat from your assumptions, not to escape them but to observe them more clearly and consider what else might be true. Perhaps a close friend, familiar with your financial circumstances, questions the wisdom of a large discretionary expense. A mentor might wonder whether your plan to step away from a role is driven by purpose or fatigue.

Returning to the earlier example of ending a long-term relationship: A friend who has been through something similar may offer both practical advice and emotional reassurance. Family members might contribute not only reassurance but also a more layered understanding of the implications. A lawyer could clarify the legal dimensions, from asset division and custody to procedural rights. Perhaps mediation offers a viable alternative?

Sometimes roles overlap. A friend may also be a lawyer, offering personal and professional insights simultaneously. Such intersections can yield perspectives that are especially grounded, neither abstract nor detached but drawn from lived experience.

Each perspective offers a distinct vantage, not a complete view but a revealing angle. The more varied the sources, the more dimensional your understanding becomes. The objective is not to achieve agreement but to sharpen discernment. In seeking out these varied voices, you may also strengthen mutual trust, invite clearer understanding, and extend the reach of empathy.

Still, these conversations can be delicate, especially when the decision touches on emotional, financial, or health-related matters. People might hesitate to recommend a different course, not only out of concern for your stability but because your decision may unsettle a balance they have come to rely on. That balance might include shared routines, unspoken agreements, or assumptions about the future that provide them with a sense of continuity or reassurance. Even subtle shifts can feel disruptive if they call existing arrangements into question. Consider, for instance, a grown child who has come to see your marriage as the stable center of the family. If you are contemplating separation, their discomfort may stem not from judgment but from uncertainty: What happens to the family holidays? What becomes of their own sense of permanence? What you experience as necessary change, they may experience as dislocation. Yet when approached with care, such exchanges can yield something rare: mutual discovery, made possible not only by what is shared but by how it is received.

Then, what matters most is how you listen. Listening well requires more than silence. It asks for real attention — to what is said, how it is said, and what may lie just beneath. Most people do not listen to understand; they listen in order to respond. But true listening offers something different. It begins with curiosity, not judgment. You might reflect back what you hear, not to endorse or rebut but to ensure mutual understanding: "So you are worried that . . ." or "It sounds like this is what matters most to you . . ." Then ask: What has led them to this view? What experiences may have shaped their concern?

Even when your perspective differs, you can still acknowledge what is real for them: "I can see why that would matter to you." That moment of recognition, however brief, creates a pause in which both people may see more clearly.

When others offer their truth, resist the reflex to correct or counter. Instead, treat their words as a mirror: not a verdict but a surface in which your own concerns may become more defined. Their view may clarify your priorities, illuminate what you had not yet considered, or reveal tensions that merit further reflection. In this way, the conversation becomes more than an exchange of opinions. It becomes a shared effort to uncover what is true.

When disagreement becomes conflict, focus on identifying shared principles or common goals. Name what you both value: sentiments like "We both desire financial stability for our family," or "Our goal is to improve communication at work." From that footing, you can move toward choices that, while not perfect, feel responsible and respectful.

The aim is not winning, nor is it about relinquishing judgment or collecting approvals. It is about preserving connection while seeking understanding and allowing wisdom to emerge through honest, considered exchange. Doing so, you are constructing a more complete understanding, one that brings together self-awareness and insight from others. As Nicholas Epley has observed, "Others' minds will never be fully accessible. The secret to understanding each other better seems to come not through an increased ability to read body language or improved perspective taking but rather through encouraging people to share their thoughts openly and honestly."[28]

That encouragement, to share, to listen, and to stay in thoughtful dialogue, is not a concession but a practice. It asks you to maintain balance amid competing views, to discern what is useful without needing to resolve every tension. When you do, you give yourself the best chance to decide wisely, not in isolation but in relation to the truth that lives between people, and the trust that grows when they are willing to share it.

Clarify Wants Versus Needs

Having taken in the perspectives of others, and listened not only to their opinions but to what their concerns reveal, turn now to your own motives. What do you want? And what do you need? If you ask a child what she wants for dinner, she might suggest a sugary treat instead of what she needs: a nutritious meal that supports her growth and development. Adults, though more sophisticated, often fall into similar patterns. We justify indulgences with thoughts like *I deserve this after such a difficult day*. By examining these impulses, you can better address the true needs behind each decision.

When considering others' viewpoints, reflect on your shared history, their unique background, and their beliefs. Compassion helps. What does their experience tell them? What are their current and future needs? What do they hope for, and what do they fear? Distinguish between what they want and what they need. For instance, someone may believe she wants a high-paying, high-powered job, but what she truly desires is a fulfilling career and to live in the city of her choosing.

The distinction between superficial wants and underlying needs is evident in both personal and group decisions. Consider, for instance, a school district debating whether to build a new sports stadium. Some community members may express enthusiasm about an initiative that increases school spirit and modernizes the campus. However, in examining the district's intentions, priorities, and long-term objectives, you may conclude that what the community truly needs is a stronger focus on improving the quality of education and ensuring fair compensation for teachers. They may be seeking a balance between extracurricular activities and the overarching mission of providing a strong academic foundation for all students.

Upon reviewing the school's financial conditions, you might discover that teachers are underpaid and the quality of basic education is declining. In this case, the community's needs may be better served by allocating resources to hiring and retaining skilled educators, updating classroom materials, and supporting teacher development rather than investing in a new sports facility. This does not necessarily mean abandoning the idea of a new stadium altogether. Decision-makers might explore partnerships with local businesses, initiate community fundraising, or apply for grants to support both educational and athletic priorities. This approach offers a way to satisfy the desire for better facilities while maintaining a commitment to educational excellence. Consider how each option might affect the broader community, including the preservation of education standards, the retention of talented teachers, and the long-term success of students. Through innovative thinking and seeking external support, it is possible to balance the ambition for improved athletic facilities and the core obligation to deliver exceptional education.

Beware of Self-Serving Endorsements

Even the most well-intentioned people you consult for advice are rarely objective. Those who care about you often aim to please. Some seek to avoid conflict. Others may not fully grasp your situation or its significance. Yet the greater risk often lies within: an unconscious desire to have your views affirmed.

In moments of uncertainty or reformation, we are often drawn to supportive voices: the people in our lives who offer affirmation, reassurance, and a sense of belonging. The feeling of not being alone matters, especially when confronting a difficult choice or trying to imagine your life in some way new. Yet even sincere encouragement can blur perspective. For those who care about you, the instinct is to comfort rather than to challenge, to offer reassurance and ease your immediate discomfort. That impulse, though well-intentioned, may come at the expense of a more discerning or long-term view.

Alternatively, their response may reflect their own history or desires. In the case of a long-term relationship coming to an end, self-serving endorsements may emerge in the advice you receive. Your close friend, recently divorced, enthusiastically supports your decision. While sincere, her encouragement likely arises from her own sense of relief or renewed independence. These feelings, valid for her, may not accurately represent your experience; they may instead reinforce the narrative of her recent choices. Meanwhile, your risk-averse parents caution against separation, emphasizing family stability. Their perspective, informed by different generational values and concern for your welfare, may underestimate your need for change. Though each view may hold some merit, both are filtered through personal history that may not align with what is right today.

Seeking perspective is not merely an exercise in gathering opinions or reinforcing your inclinations. Rather, it is a means of moving beyond bias, yours and theirs, to bring into view the full range of needs, obligations, and consequences that each decision carries.

A useful example can be found in something as ordinary as dining out. Consider the approach of a skilled server. When asked for a recommendation, some respond with a personal favorite: "Try the duck," or "I like the vichyssoise." In contrast, the best servers begin by asking what you enjoy. Do you typically prefer red meat or fish? Do you lean toward vegetarian dishes? They ask about dietary restrictions: Are there any allergies to consider? They gauge your appetite. How hungry are you? Are you looking for something to share?

Similarly, the most effective advisors, like the attentive server, do not assume there is one best option. Even when pressed, they are reluctant to recommend without first placing themselves in your position. They begin with thoughtful questions, aiming to discern what might be right for you. This approach ensures their guidance speaks to the present moment while honoring the longer arc of your life.

Most advice, whether it affirms your current thinking or presents a different point of view, contains an embedded meaning. For instance, when discussing a financial decision with a trusted advisor, he or she may offer specific guidance on saving or investing. These suggestions may offer practical value, but the greater insight often lies in the principle behind them. The underlying message might concern responsibility, delayed gratification, or preparation for uncertainty.

Once you have solicited someone's response, pause to consider the broader message. Then try to distill it to its essence. Can you express their advice in a few words or a single sentence? By discerning that underlying theme, you can apply what is useful while setting aside what is not. Understanding does not require agreement. It may be wise to save every dollar for tomorrow. But what about the joy a few dollars exchanged for meaningful experiences could bring today?

Friends, family, and even a thoughtful server may offer guidance, each in their own way. The essential task is to seek out perspectives, especially those that differ from your own. Only then can you turn to the more consequential question: Does this apply to your life as it is or as you wish it to be?

Objective and perceptive advisors may not offer answers that feel immediately reassuring, but they often offer what proves most valuable over time. A contrasting view, formed through different experiences, can expose gaps in your reasoning and bring into view truths you may not have seen alone.

What Do They Not Know That Could Affect Their Response?

Having considered others' perspectives and potential biases, we turn to an equally important question: What information might they be missing?

Just as those we think we know best can sometimes surprise us, we often remain a mystery even to ourselves. Our preferences, beliefs, and motivations evolve over time, often without our full awareness. Tastes that once defined us may lose their appeal. Reflecting on our youth, we might question past enthusiasms for songs, activities, or styles that now seem out of place.

Given this constant change and variety of influences, it is unrealistic to expect others, even those closest to us, to know us entirely or understand the full extent of our motives and desires today. These people may be affected by our choices, but they can see us only from their perspective.

The role of information, both shared and withheld, influences the advice we receive. Consider the context in which someone offers guidance: What might they not know? What are you reluctant to admit? Even those who know you well — a longtime friend, a colleague who respects you, someone who has loved you for years — can offer only what your words allow. If you speak openly about feeling unfulfilled at work, they may respond not just with encouragement but with support that reflects what you are genuinely seeking: a clearer sense of direction, creative freedom, or a sense of alignment between what you do and who you are. If, instead, you remain vague or guarded, the advice you receive may feel incomplete or misdirected.

Often, we hesitate to speak plainly because doing so would require revealing something tender, inconvenient, or difficult to justify. You may feel an urge to leave your career entirely to pursue something that feels meaningful but impractical, such as writing, music, or teaching. Or perhaps you are drawn to a different city but dread upsetting your family by moving away. You might feel torn between holding onto a beloved routine — a hobby, a community, an identity — and making a decision that demands its sacrifice. These omissions, however understandable, can create a distance between what you need and what others can offer.

Shared, complete information is essential. If we want sound advice, we must first invite others into our world. This means offering more than a list of facts or a recounting of events. We must also reveal the parts of ourselves that often remain hidden: the desires, hesitations, doubts, and hopes that so often direct us. By presenting a full and honest account, we provide the context others need to offer counsel that is both relevant and considered. Only then can we begin to integrate what we know about ourselves with what others may help us recognize.

Just as a tree draws strength from roots that reach far below the surface, we are sustained by an interior life that must be both acknowledged and expressed. But a tree does not remain beneath the earth. It grows upward and outward. In the same way, we must look beyond ourselves and remain open to what others may help us see. Our choices become less reactive and more deliberate. We create the conditions in which meaningful growth can occur, rooted in what is true while reaching toward the light.

Summary

Chapter 5, "Seek Perspective" emphasizes that no meaningful decision exists in isolation. Every choice reaches beyond the individual, touching people whose lives are linked to your own in ways that are easy to overlook. Seeking perspective asks you to widen your view and consider how a decision may be experienced by others. It calls for asking questions that examine what your own viewpoint leaves out. When decisions are approached this way, they rest on a more complete understanding of what follows from them and what is owed to those affected. As you reflect on this chapter, consider the following questions:

1. Whose decisions have most influenced your life up to this point, directly or indirectly?

2. What types of decisions do you typically seek others' advice on, and whom do you turn to?

3. What tends to limit your willingness to consider perspectives that differ from your own?

4. What information is often missing when people offer guidance, and why does that absence matter?

5. When asked to help someone else make a decision, how might personal interests or past experience influence your response?

Challenges

Self-Discovery: Choose a decision you are considering now. List the individuals or groups likely to be affected. For each, write two brief lines: what they may want, and what they may fear or resist. Then ask: Which perspective most challenges your current leaning, and what information might be missing from your view?

Further Exploration: Choose one person meaningfully affected by the outcome. State your question plainly and invite their perspective: "What do you notice here that I may not?" Listen without rebuttal or explanation. Afterward, write down (1) what you learned and (2) what surprised you. What is one piece of information you should share or seek before deciding?

Chapter 6 — Envision Someone Wise

It is the barely-visible stars which sharpen our eyesight.
—Henry Stanley Haskins

As important as it is to consider the viewpoints of those most affected by your choice, the counsel of a wise, impartial individual can be equally enlightening.

Imagine you could seek advice from one person concerning your quandary, someone who is removed from the immediate influence of your decision yet still cares about how the outcome will affect everyone involved. This could be anyone you respect for their wisdom: a historical figure, a renowned expert, a character from literature, an acquaintance who consistently demonstrates sound judgment, or even a future, wiser version of yourself.

If you could summon one advisor, a sage, to guide your decision, who would it be?

Perhaps you already have someone in mind, someone whose advice has helped you overcome challenges or see situations more clearly. How did their guidance influence your choices, actions, or the person you have become? This exercise invites you to reflect on those voices and explore who might offer the most valuable insights now.

Regardless of whom you envision, remember that their wisdom often lies not in providing ready-made solutions but in encouraging exploration of the question itself. Perhaps you already know the answer, or maybe you need to investigate further to achieve the clarity you seek.

While this chapter focuses on seeking guidance from one individual, wisdom often emerges from various sources, each contributing to a broader understanding. Whomever you turn to for counsel, concentrate on the thought-provoking questions they might ask.

Sometimes, the best way forward is to step back and consider: What would a truly wise person inquire about?

Personal Account: Part Four

After gathering opinions from those affected by my potential decision, I remained concerned that I might overlook important considerations. Who else could provide counsel? I needed someone experienced who could offer an objective perspective, someone outside my family, friends, or peers. Since I had no affiliations with any faith communities, religious leaders like bishops, rabbis, or lamas were not options, and there were no clear role models in my family. In a departure from my usual problem-solving approaches, I sought guidance from an executive coach named Phil. Our partnership evolved into a transformative mentorship that influenced my daily life and decisions beyond.

Phil coached entrepreneurs and executives while training to become a Buddhist monk. With his round body, shaved head, and cherubic face, he resembled a modern Laughing Buddha.[29] He also embodied the ideal that wisdom can come in various forms: Despite lacking legal or business expertise, Phil proved an exceptional mentor. He excelled at active listening, posing probing questions, and encouraging me to think more expansively. Like any good teacher, Phil appeared committed to my well-being and was quick to guide me when he sensed I might be going astray.

At this juncture, my life was veering off course. My working relationship with George was in a downward spiral that Phil astutely labeled toxic. George noted my growing detachment from the legal profession and our shared life. The implication was clear: Our decade-long partnership was at the precipice of dissolution. Meanwhile, our increasingly neglected firm descended into chaos, resembling a cautionary tale. The firm's decline manifested at every level of our organization. One of our attorneys entered rehabilitation for alcohol abuse. The support staff operated under continuous strain, their usual efficiency and collegiality replaced by tension and uncertainty. Communication between George and me had deteriorated to the point where we barely exchanged words. His drinking had begun to encroach into the workday, to a point where he was adding whiskey to his morning coffee. In my way, I was also unraveling — as I began an extramarital affair.

As much as I longed for immediate solutions, Phil demurred from offering easy answers. Knowing that significant life choices must stem from one's fundamental purpose, he sought to provoke self-reflection instead of suggesting a particular course of action. His questions — "What truly matters to you?" and "What is driving your desire for change?" — centered less on making a change and more on questioning the reasons for being on any path at all.

While these questions may seem obvious now, they were far from my immediate concerns. Phil's guidance led to a period of introspection and a reevaluation of priorities. Was I trading dollars for days or investing in my future? Was a new career the true means of fulfillment? This process helped me look past superficial dilemmas and toward the underlying motivations for pursuing law. In time, the insights that emerged compelled me to define what I value, establish guiding principles, and articulate a purpose. It prompted a more honest examination of my strengths, interests, and desires, and how I might use them to serve the community in a meaningful way.

My motivations for pursuing law — the challenge, a belief in justice, or financial reward — seemed important enough. Through my dialogues with Phil, however, I realized they did not capture the entirety of my aspirations. What attracted me to business was the opportunity to build an enterprise with lasting, positive influence, an endeavor that included challenge, reflected justice, and reached far beyond what I, as a lawyer, could accomplish alone. One might think the nonprofit sector would be a logical next step; however, nonprofits are no less immune to dysfunction than any other organization. I wanted to stretch my boundaries, work collaboratively with a team, take on larger challenges, and contribute to something that would have a lasting, positive effect beyond my direct involvement.

Phil's guidance was critical beyond this specific circumstance; it sparked a transformation that redefined my decision-making and life. He instilled in me that pursuing wisdom is a never-ending process. If we trust ourselves and each other, every person, situation, and decision offers something: a new perspective, a fresh idea, or a better way. He helped me articulate the intentions and aspirations that formed the blueprint for the life I wanted to lead.

Now, when confronted with challenges or opportunities, I reflect on Phil's question: "Why does *this* matter to you?" He later sharpened it to: "How does this align with your values and intentions?" This question has become a touchstone, aligning my choices and actions with who I am and aim to be. It reminds me to live consciously, ensuring each decision is a deliberate choice aligned with my core intentions and aspirations.

And the question behind all questions? For Phil, it was simple: "How will you end suffering?"

Let Your Mind Wander — the Choices Are Limitless

Envisioning a wise person is an exercise in limitless imagination, transcending all boundaries. This person might be someone you admire, aspire to emulate, or even create in your imagination. He or she could emerge from a broad range of traditions or disciplines: from religious figures like Jesus, the Prophet Mohammad, or the Dalai Lama to luminaries in business, philosophy, politics, science, literature, or even sports.

Let your vision remain open. Not having met someone does not prevent you from envisioning his or her enlightened approach to life's challenges.

Take Socrates, who famously argued that no one knowingly chooses to do wrong and that true understanding requires precise definition. This thought process, known as the Socratic Paradox, is often associated with the principle *I know one thing; that I know nothing.*[30] Recognizing what you do not know can spark the desire to learn, an essential step toward wisdom.

The wise person you envision could also be a character from literature, cinema, or drama. For instance, Athena from *The Odyssey*, Atticus Finch from *To Kill a Mockingbird*, or the fox from *The Little Prince*. These figures often embody virtues like confronting adversity with bravery, showing empathy and selflessness, adhering steadfastly to their intentions, and acting with honor and sincerity. These qualities, desirable in any mentor, can be found in a variety of sources.[31]

However, if visualizing the wisdom of someone unknown to you feels challenging, consider the wisdom of people you know. These could be leaders in your community, close friends, or acquaintances. Throughout our lives, we encounter many humble people who leave a lasting impression on everyone they meet. The goal is to broaden your perspective beyond your current sphere.

In this context, the wise person you envision could even be your future self a decade or two down the line. As you ponder wisdom, a wiser version of yourself is undoubtedly emerging. With the lessons learned today, you will continue to accrue wisdom in the days ahead. Your future self, armed with experiences and foresight, can warn you of impending obstacles or reflect on the past to help you approach the present with greater understanding. After all, you understand yourself better than anyone.

As children, we are taught that wisdom is an attribute of older generations. As we mature, our understanding of wisdom evolves. A wise person might be someone with exceptional expertise in a specific field or who has undergone experiences like those you are contemplating.

When the wisdom of those you know proves insufficient, or if your future self remains silent, consider the qualities that define true wisdom. Wise individuals assess troubling situations objectively, listen actively, delay their responses, and avoid hasty judgments influenced by emotional bias. They critically evaluate all facets of an issue, prioritize others' concerns, and combine this with real-world problem-solving skills.

Moreover, wise individuals respond to ambiguity with ease, balancing knowledge and doubt. They act when situations are within their control and accept their inability to do so when circumstances are beyond their reach. They seek balanced solutions, consider conflicting interests, and recognize that the appropriateness of actions depends on context: time, place, and circumstances.

At this point, you should have identified the wise individual you wish to emulate. With your problem in mind, it is time to consider the questions they might ask. Imagining a conversation with them will help you organize your thoughts. What aspects of the problem would you choose to reveal? Which ones would you omit?

In this hypothetical dialogue, avoid asking them *What would you do if you were me?* This question is unhelpful, as it assumes the wise individual understands all aspects of your problem and can guide you toward one decision or another. However, solutions are rarely so straightforward.

Instead, relax into the silence. Silence embodies wisdom itself, reflecting their attentive engagement with your predicament. It invites you to attune to your environment, first focusing on yourself and then expanding your awareness of your surroundings. This concentrated attention stirs empathy within you, generating a sense of ease and allowing you to examine the issue with greater tranquility. As you envision the wise individual contemplating your predicament in thoughtful silence, your whirlwind of thoughts begins to subside. This exercise is not about finding immediate answers but fostering a mindset that invites understanding and introspection. It is about exploring the potent questions these figures might pose and the wisdom those questions can unlock.

What Questions Might a Wise Person Ask?

Consulting a wise person rarely yields an immediate response. This is not because they lack an initial inclination, nor because they intend to evade. Rather, it is because the hallmark of wise counsel is not certainty but humility. They understand the limits of what they may know. *Tell me more*, they might begin. Although this approach can stir frustration, particularly when what you seek is a definitive conclusion, they recognize that answering too quickly risks sending you in the wrong direction. As important still, it may deprive you of the opportunity to arrive at an answer through your own effort, thereby bypassing the very process through which discernment takes form.

Every decision is framed by unspoken considerations: unexamined assumptions, practical constraints, and the ongoing negotiation of identity. These are matters an outside observer cannot fully perceive. Thus, the role of a wise person is not to offer reassurance or resolution. Rather, they remain an attentive companion as you venture into places you might not otherwise go and prompt you to envision perspectives you might not otherwise see.

Consider a question that arises for many in their work: whether to pursue an advanced degree or professional certification. Perhaps it is preparation for a field you hope to enter or a means of advancing your standing in the work you already do. You seek out someone whose judgment you trust, perhaps a colleague further along in your profession or someone known to offer sound advice. You pose your question, hoping for a definitive answer. Instead, she begins by examining your assumptions. Is the degree still regarded as essential, or has the field evolved to place greater value on experience?

She may then turn to practical considerations, asking whether your interest arises from a desire for substantive education or whether you regard the degree as a safeguard, something to list on a résumé to ease a lingering concern. She may raise questions about cost. What would you need to give up in order to make it possible? And what do you expect to receive in return? As you respond, she listens closely, not only to what you say but to how you speak. And if you begin to retreat into abstraction, she presses you to be specific. What would this mean for your time, your resources, and the future you are trying to create?

Finally, she may turn the question back on itself. If someone you cared about brought you this same dilemma, what would you ask the person to consider? What guidance would you offer? It is often easier to offer sound advice to another than to arrive at it for oneself. By assuming the role of advisor, or by imagining the decision from a temporal point further away in time, the matter can come into view with greater objectivity. How much will this decision matter in a week, a month, or a year?

These questions are not intended to delay the choice. Rather, they are meant to clarify what you believe you know, what you truly understand, and what may still lie beyond your reach. Wisdom does not reside in the possession of any single answer but in the discipline of learning to ask the questions. Some may be answered in the moment; others are meant to remain with you and be reexamined over time. Through this process, the wise person encourages curiosity, fosters understanding, and helps you arrive at the answer that is right for you.

Perhaps you will determine that the degree is not worth the financial burden or the time it would require. Or perhaps you will come to see that the accomplishment holds meaning apart from any practical return. In either case, by imagining a dialogue with such a person and beginning to hear their voice within your own reflections, you are not merely resolving a single matter. You are internalizing their wisdom. And with that capacity comes the realization that, at times, responding too quickly risks leaving concealed something more consequential than the question itself.

What Is the Question Behind the Question?

At the heart of nearly every persistent dilemma lies a more funda-mental concern. The struggle to choose, or the discomfort that persists, may be a signal that the matter at hand is bound to some-thing more elemental. The unease itself gestures toward something we might hesitate to acknowledge: that there is a more fundamental question behind the question.

For instance, the question *Should I accept this job offer?* might conceal more important inquiries. Nested within it reside deeper concerns such as *What kind of work holds meaning for me? What am I uniquely suited to do?* or *What direction do I want my life to take?* These are not distractions. They are signals.

That is why the wise do not move quickly to resolve. They listen not only to what is said but also to what remains unsaid. They notice the words you hesitate to speak, the thoughts you leave unfinished. Their inquiry does not impose a verdict. Instead, it offers a place to pause, press in, and begin to consider what has not yet been fully brought into view. They help you stay with the matter long enough to notice its edges and the tensions that remain unresolved. In this way, inquiry becomes more than analysis. It becomes an encounter with the self.

What lies behind the original dilemma often concerns the more elusive matters we hesitate to name, such as who you are, what you value, or what you are in the process of becoming. These are not matters of convenience. Rather, they are questions of meaning or value. They require discernment and often ask more of us than we wish to give. Yet until they are acknowledged, a sense of uncertainty remains. What begins as a decision about whether to take a particular job may reappear, later and differently worded, as whether to accept a project, change course, or leave the field altogether.

To articulate these fundamental inquiries, whatever form they take, is not to resolve them. It is to bring them into view. And that, in itself, is the first step toward progress. It draws a line between what tugs at your attention and the more pressing matter of what you must attend to. Gradually, your posture aligns. You move from reaction toward intention. You begin not simply to answer what has been asked but to understand why it was asked at all.

This is the true gift of wise counsel. They do not answer for you. They help you uncover the fundamental concern that lingers behind the one you have voiced, the one you may be unaware of, reluctant to name, or still working to understand. And when you begin to raise such matters without prompting, when you pause to consider not only the decision but your relationship to it, you enter the labor that precedes all wisdom: the effort to know yourself. You become, for yourself, a source of equanimity. Not certain but honest. And that is where the real work begins.

Summary

Chapter 6, "Envision Someone Wise," invites you to step beyond the viewpoints of those directly involved and consider counsel from a figure you regard as wise and impartial. That figure need not be distant or extraordinary. There may be many people around you who, in their unique ways, are sources of wisdom. A wise person tends to slow the pace, ask for context, test assumptions, and direct attention to what you may be avoiding. Often, that inquiry reveals a more fundamental concern behind the one you first named. In time, this practice helps you hear a wiser voice within your own thinking and strengthens your ability to advise yourself and others with care. As you reflect on this chapter, consider the following questions:

1. Who is someone you would turn to when facing an important decision, and why?

2. What qualities or habits of thought make this person a source of wise counsel for you?

3. How might speaking with this person help you see beyond your immediate concerns?

4. What questions do you imagine this person would ask before offering advice?

5. How might their counsel change the way you approach decisions, especially when you feel pressed to respond quickly?

Challenges

Self-Discovery: Identify one person you regard as wise (a mentor, an elder, a historical figure, or your future self). Bring to mind a decision that has remained unresolved. On one page, write the questions that person would ask before you act. Keep them pointed and specific. Then answer each question in your own voice, without explanation or defense. Conclude with one sentence that names what now seems most important.

Further Exploration. Arrange a brief conversation with someone whose judgment you respect. Present the decision in no more than a few sentences, then invite this prompt: "What question would you want me to answer before deciding?" Allow them to respond fully. Follow by exploring why that question matters. Afterward, write down the question and your response to it. Note how this exchange influenced your understanding of the decision.

Chapter 7 — Engage the Voice of Wisdom

What . . . is Truth? A difficult question; but I have solved it for myself by saying that it is what the voice within tells you.
—Mahatma Gandhi[32]

Some years ago, *Rolling Stone*, the influential music and culture magazine, set out to review the history of jazz, ranking every recording released to that point on a scale of one to five stars. The comprehensive guide encompassed more than four thousand albums. The editors included an important caveat in its preface: "A three-star record from a marginal player is probably not as good as a three-star record from a genius,"[33] meaning even a seemingly average Miles Davis album — one they may have assigned two, three, or even four stars — was exceptional compared to that of almost any other artist. After all, this was Miles Davis, whose albums included *In a Silent Way* and *Kind of Blue* — masterpieces for the ages.

We carry within us an internal wisdom that, when protected from myriad external influences, can surpass even the most well-intentioned advice, because we know ourselves better than anyone. A multitude of sources bombard us with advice on how to live, from popular philosophies and charismatic leaders to cultural trends and societal expectations. We are often drawn to these role models or techniques, not merely because they appear relatable or promise quick solutions but because they offer the illusion of certainty in an uncertain world. Yet, amid the clamor of external voices, it is easy to forget that the most reliable guidance often comes from within — a wisdom uniquely attuned to our individual lives.

Here is a truth worth recognizing: Only you can accurately gauge what you are capable of. You alone possess complete knowledge of your history, true motivations, and innermost desires. Consequently, the answers that matter most must come from within.

To be genuinely healthy, happy, or successful, we must undertake the demanding task of understanding ourselves. At first, we may think the solution lies in applying reason or intuition to our choices. However, relying solely on intellect can distance us from what is truly essential, while intuition alone might obscure rational considerations. True self-knowledge requires more than either approach in isolation. This process requires a willingness to set aside preconceived notions about identity and question fundamental assumptions about meaning and success. It calls for us to pause and turn inward, to reconnect with that inner reservoir of wisdom, the part of us that knows: the voice of wisdom.

The voice of wisdom weaves together the threads of our past, present, and future. Yet how often do we truly listen? Ignoring or turning away from this wisdom invites a life of quiet desperation, confined in unfulfilling lifestyles or careers, as the shadows of our true ambitions gradually fade.

But there is another way. When we attune ourselves to the wisdom expressed through this voice, each decision feels intrinsically right. A succession of these aligned choices brings clarity, lightness, and a sense of purpose. The result? A life enriched by wisdom, where every day fulfills the promise of both accomplishment and meaning — a life truly worth living.

The Voice of Wisdom: Its Origin and Purpose

As you engage with the voice of wisdom, a question may naturally arise: *Where does this wisdom come from?* Is it a divine entity, nature, a cosmic force, the universe, or an aspect of our consciousness? This is a question that resists certainty, one that may forever remain shrouded in mystery, much like contemplating the vastness of the universe or the mechanics of time. Whatever its source, the purpose of the voice of wisdom remains clear: *to ensure your health, happiness, and success.*

Wisdom itself flows through all living beings. We observe it in the natural world around us, in how trees grow toward the light or animals migrate south in the winter. While a multitude of voices exists within us — reason, compassion, intuition, fear, anger, determination, and self-doubt, among others — the voice of wisdom does not utter a sound. Unlike these other voices, to *hear* is to encounter a sense of *knowing* that permeates our being, one that precedes conscious thought. It might manifest as a sudden flash of insight, illuminating the way forward, or surface gradually as a subtle inclination, gently steering us back on course.

If we were to break down the voice of wisdom into a *why* and a *how*, we could say this: Its *why* ensures our well-being, while its *how* operates on three levels: first, by helping us perceive what is true; second, by enabling us to conceive what is right; and third, by subtly guiding us to respond appropriately in the moment. This process aligns our actions with our highest good. However, to benefit from this wisdom, we must actively engage with it by listening intently. This means quieting the clamor of our everyday thoughts to receive the calm, clear direction emanating from this voice.

Think of it this way: You are walking through an unfamiliar forest, captivated by the beauty of towering trees and vibrant foliage. As you meander along winding paths, taking in the sights and sounds of nature, you become disoriented and suddenly realize you have lost your bearings. The dense canopy obscures familiar landmarks. Panic sets in as you notice the sun is setting, casting long shadows through the trees. You begin to worry about being stuck in the wilderness after dark. To find your way back, you must stop, quiet your racing thoughts, and listen carefully for the sound of a distant stream or observe the position of the fading sun through gaps in the leaves. In this moment of stillness, you allow your senses to attune to the subtle cues around you — the direction of the breeze, the slope of the land, the calls of birds — guiding you toward safety and familiar territory before nightfall.

Listening intently to the voice of wisdom requires a similar focus. Doing so opens us to guidance that transcends our limited perspective and taps into a broader understanding. When we fail to pause and consult this wisdom, we often react from a place of fear, a product of our survival instinct. Alternatively, we might approach situations from a mindset of *already knowing*, forfeiting the opportunity to learn something new or essential for understanding the present.

If you have not heard this voice, do not worry. No matter how long you may have ignored it, the voice of wisdom is always there, patiently waiting to offer guidance. To reconnect with this wisdom, you need only pause and turn inward. This process might involve moments of quiet reflection, mindful breathing, or simply allowing yourself to be still. Then, gently place your awareness at the center of your being. Here, in this place, you can reconnect with the wisdom flowing through and around you.

When we engage with it, the voice of wisdom illuminates the truth and rightness of our actions, revealing the consequences of each choice. For instance, when considering a new job opportunity, your mind might assess the financial benefits or evaluate how the position aligns with your intentions and career objectives. However, the voice of wisdom prompts you to consider the broader effects of your choice: how it might alter your daily routines, influence your relationships, and contribute to your long-term fulfillment. Disregarding this wisdom may result in choices that undermine your overall well-being and long-term satisfaction.

The challenge of truly reconnecting with this inner guidance is universal. We live in a world saturated with noise and interference, factors both internal and external that muffle the voice of wisdom. Even now, as I write, the hum of a fan, the buzz of a computer, and the distant roar of an airplane press against the edges of my awareness, subtle intrusions that remind me how easily the connection is lost.

Adding to this is the continuous stream of thoughts about tasks, responsibilities, and the countless stimuli vying for our attention. There is also the temptation to disengage, to passively be entertained, or simply consume. These interruptions, which often seem urgent or alluring, draw us away from the raw experience of the present and our connection to the wisdom within.

Patience is critical. Like any skill, learning to engage the voice of wisdom requires practice and dedication. To the inexperienced traveler, the night sky presents a bewildering array of indistinguishable lights. In contrast, a seasoned voyager confidently charts their course by a single star amidst the vast expanse. While, at first, identifying that guiding light might be difficult, with time and practice, it becomes instinctive. Eventually, this reflective practice becomes an integral part of who you are.

Personal Account: Part Five

From an early age, I lived by the quintessential achiever's ethos: Set ambitious goals, work tirelessly, and — someday! — rewards will follow. This cultural narrative promises success in exchange for time and effort. Happiness lies just beyond the next accomplishment, like a mirage shimmering on the horizon. Without questioning, I accepted this as truth. My relentless drive for achievement consumed me. Every aspect of my life became an opportunity for optimization, from maximizing productivity at work to meticulously planning my personal time around peak experiences.

This pursuit aligned with my personality traits. While I resist categorizing human behavior, I acknowledge we all have innate preferences. Personality assessments, such as the Myers-Briggs Type Indicator, highlight my predisposition toward introversion and logic. My mind naturally gravitates toward analysis, promising mastery over life's complexities. This analytical approach has served me throughout my career, from the abstract realm of mathematics in school to synthesizing legal cases into coherent narratives for judges and juries. This logical approach seemed like a direct route to success.

Yet, over the years, a subtle disquiet grew within me. Despite systematically checking off goals on the list, I found myself questioning why I was not happy. Following traditional vectors of success only brought conditional, fleeting happiness. Hours grew longer, benchmarks rose higher, and the cycle felt endless, as if winning a pie-eating contest was rewarded with . . . yet more pie.

The pursuit of success, once exhilarating, now felt burdensome. Increasingly, I found myself staring at a page for extended periods, wondering if there was something more. In time, an awareness emerged: While my habitual analytical reasoning excelled at structured problem-solving, it often proved inadequate when confronting decisions, personal or profound. I needed a different kind of intelligence — one grounded in reason yet attuned to my emotional states — to guide the way forward. This realization would eventually lead me to discover what I would call the voice of wisdom.

Meanwhile, the pressures of modern life — meeting deadlines, nurturing social connections, and responding to the constant influx of communication — felt unrelenting. I toiled for days, disregarding clear signs of physical and emotional strain. Meeting work objectives alone was demanding, yet the world continually demanded more. My body and heart sent clear signals, if only I had paused to heed them. I was a knot of tension, with taut muscles, shallow breathing, and a collapsing posture. Many nights, I retired beneath a shroud of exhaustion, emotionally drained. Where was the time to reassess my priorities?

Eventually, the question of a career change reached a critical point. The lease on the law office approached renewal, and the prospect of taking on new clients while doubting my commitment to the profession felt increasingly unethical. External forces imposed a deadline, compelling me to make a decision; I felt an urgent need for resolution. Yet a substantial part of me resisted. Uncertainty lingered, manifesting in sleepless nights and restless days filled with indecision.

In the brief interludes when I contemplated transitioning from the law, a chorus of internal voices emerged. Some questioned surrendering a professional identity, others whispered of the allure of new challenges, while still others warned of the risks of change. Amidst this mental clamor, I had long sought refuge in activities like running, bicycling, or motorcycle riding.

If you have participated in sports or similar activities, you may understand the sensation. Such pursuits, with their intensity and, often, inherent risks, demand your complete attention. The rest of life and any attendant worries simply fall away.

It was akin to that moment on a motorcycle when you fully trust the machine. Entering a curve, you lean your body forward and down directly toward the asphalt. The bike pitches sideways, and the world skims past just below. The wind buffeting your helmet suddenly dissipates as a pocket of air forms around you. Amidst the swirling noise and wind, you experience an abiding sense of presence, purpose, and ultimately peace — a perfect singularity. Your mind becomes completely clear, achieving a state beyond words. As you reach the apex, you pull back on the throttle. The bike's power surges, lifting you upright and pressing you firmly into the seat as you go streaking down the highway.

While such pursuits offer temporary respite from the ceaseless distractions of the day, they cannot reliably provide answers. In fact, we often engage in these activities to escape from the questions. They serve as a gateway to approaches better suited for life-altering choices.

I needed to look within. Like riding a twisting highway, I had to let everything else go. Allow the thoughts — desire, ambition, doubt, reason, fear, and judgment — to fade. Instead, I returned to a state of stillness. In this quietude, I could sink beneath the surface chatter of my mind to rediscover the center of my being: not a physical location but a state of pure awareness. Here, the distinction between self and other dissolved, leaving only consciousness observing itself. A moment of simply being.

In that instant, the answer became clear: Law was no longer my path. The work had turned monotonous, and I felt stuck. Each passing day pulled me further from the future I desired. In that moment, a new realm of possibilities unfolded, and the direction I needed to pursue became undeniable.

Having experienced this space at the center of my being, how might I describe it? It feels like returning home, to a sanctuary within myself. In this place, my body unwinds, my heart reconnects with the people and places around me, and my mind reclaims a sense of purpose. With each return, the path reveals itself more clearly, and the choice to follow it becomes more deliberate. Within this inner sanctuary, I discover the voice of wisdom, an ever-present force communicating through every aspect of my being.

This voice of wisdom offers more than mere answers; it instills confidence in discerning what is right. It serves as a reliable guide for meaningful decisions and in moments when I seek peace. My growing attentiveness to this inner voice offers orientation when choices feel uncertain. It serves as an ongoing reminder to live consciously. As I attune to it, my choices align more closely with my intentions and aspirations, enriching my experiences and my interactions with others.

This voice of wisdom also resides in you. It has always been present, illuminating your consciousness. Consider, for instance, when you were five years old and perhaps wondered if taking money from your mother's purse was acceptable. The voice reminded you of the consequences. At thirty-five, as you ponder the nature of your work and question its fulfillment, this same voice provides an answer.

While questions evolve, so do you. Each experience enriches your understanding and strengthens your ability to engage with your inner wisdom. Success, once trivial at age ten, may crystallize as a goal at twenty or thirty. By sixty? It might symbolize personal significance. Irrespective of your age or stage in life, the voice of wisdom remains a steadfast companion.

Engaging the Voice of Wisdom

Engaging the voice of wisdom involves three essential steps: pause, turn inward to locate the center of your being, and listen. While simple in concept, these steps require practice and dedication to master.

1. Pause

Pausing is the first step to wisdom and the gateway to true freedom. Between action and reaction lies a vast expanse. Within this space resides our power to choose our thoughts, words, and actions, shaping our responses and, ultimately, our lives. Yet we rarely receive instruction on mastering this seemingly simple act.

To pause means precisely that: to cease doing. Or, as the clever refrain suggests: Do not just do something; stand there. This seemingly paradoxical advice reminds us to resist the urge for immediate action and instead create space for thoughtful consideration. Pausing is more than a brief interruption in activity; it is a deliberate disengagement from the flow of thoughts, emotions, and external stimuli that typically occupy our attention. Like a tree standing resolute amid a storm, its roots stretching deep into the earth, pausing allows us to stay grounded as the chaos of daily life swirls around us.

The conditions for an effective pause can differ based on the situation and the time available. In a heated argument, you might pause even for a few seconds to regain composure. In contrast, you may take days or weeks to deliberate during a major life decision. This practice might initially feel unfamiliar, even uncomfortable, as we have become accustomed to constant motion and stimulation. However, with consistent practice, pausing becomes more natural and rewarding.

To incorporate the practice of pausing into your life, consider these steps:

a. **Find a quiet environment.** Whenever possible, select a place to sit or lie down comfortably without distractions. This environment should be conducive to relaxation and concentration. However, remember that a pause can happen anywhere, even in a noisy environment, by focusing inward.

b. **Adopt a comfortable posture.** Whether sitting or lying down, ensure that your posture is stable and relaxed. The spine should be straight to facilitate unobstructed breathing and circulation. If you cannot change your posture, simply become aware of your body's position.

c. **Close your eyes.** When circumstances allow, closing your eyes helps shut out visual distractions to focus on the internal experience. If closing your eyes is not feasible, gently lower your gaze to minimize external visual input.

d. **Breathe deeply.** Begin by taking a few full breaths. Inhale slowly and deeply through the nose, allowing the abdomen to rise, and exhale gently through the mouth. This practice helps calm your nervous system and anchors your attention to the present moment. Even a single mindful breath can serve as a powerful pause.

e. **Acknowledge your thoughts.** As you pause, you may become aware of thoughts that arise. Instead of engaging with them, acknowledge their presence and let them pass. This practice of nonattachment is essential for achieving mindful awareness, allowing you to observe without becoming entangled.

The power of pausing lies not in its duration but in the quality of attention it promotes. Whether you have a few minutes or just a heartbeat, pausing is about redirecting your focus from external distractions to your inner experience. This attentiveness can transform even the briefest interlude into a moment of complete presence, allowing you to access your inner wisdom and make more thoughtful decisions.

Begin integrating this practice into your daily life by starting small. When you feel anxious, fearful, or overwhelmed by a strong negative emotion, such as anger, jealousy, or unhealthy desire, stop whatever you are doing. This alone can help prevent emotions from escalating and allow for more thoughtful responses. Take a breath. Permit yourself just to be.

To create a consistent habit, consider setting intentional moments throughout your day for this practice. Tie it to your existing routine to redirect yourself from negative thoughts. This could be linked to certain times of day, such as early morning as you begin your day, before starting a meal, or just before bed. You might anchor yourself to a specific physical space, such as when entering a room or taking an evening walk. Alternatively, connect the practice to a physical object like a photograph, meaningful item, or piece of jewelry.

Even a brief pause can calm the mind. Instead of reacting, stop. Resist the reflex to respond. Take one mindful breath, then another. If possible, change your physical position. Stand. Step outside. Walk for a few minutes without searching for an answer. Allow the surface agitation to subside on its own.

Return to this again and again. Over time, the pause requires less effort. It becomes familiar. Then it becomes reliable. Gradually, reactivity loosens its hold and mental chatter fades into the background. In that opening, impulse no longer directs you. You are prepared to return to center.

2. Center

Building on the practice of pausing and centering yourself enables you to access a state of undivided awareness and connection. To center your awareness, let yourself gradually sink beneath your thoughts like a stone gently descending through still water. Begin by noticing your quietest thought, then the next quietest thought. Continue to trace this line persistently until all the noise subsides.

Remind yourself that, in this moment, nothing is more important. As other thoughts drift through your mind — your to-do list, your wants, needs, desires, your bias to action — do not worry. Simply let them drift away, knowing they will still be there later. Releasing these thoughts opens up space for insight and understanding. You cannot stop these distractions, but you can remain present as they pass.

Now, direct your attention to the center of your being, where your breath naturally flows in and out. If you need a physical point of reference, consider the solar plexus — the body's center, named for the Sun. Feel its warmth.

As you remain centered, imagine standing at the entrance of a shrine, temple, sacred space, or some other place where you experience peace and feel connected to your surroundings. This might be a familiar beach, a spot in nature, or a landscape that exists only in your imagination, such as a secluded cove or warm campfire. Engage all your senses by turn: Feel the air on your skin, hear the ambient sounds, notice the scents around you, and take in what is in your range of sight.

Enter this space, whatever form it takes — light or dark, warm or cool, colorful or muted — choosing the environment where you feel most at ease. In this space, dualities (such as good/bad, you/them, or this/that) dissolve, leaving only an open expanse of pure awareness resting in itself: a return to home.

Here, *home* refers not to a physical location but to the center of your being, the inner sanctuary within yourself. It is where the layers of identity and ego, the external personas we construct, fall away, revealing your authentic self. The you that embodies health and happiness and is fully awake. The you that feels peace-filled, loving, and loved. The you that perceives beauty, truth, and goodness in everyone and everything. The you that meets change with courage, compassion, and grace, allowing wisdom to guide your thoughts, words, and actions.

3. Listen

Once centered, you are ready to listen with the entirety of your being. In this eternal abode, at the center of your being, the process of inquiry begins. Free from the distractions, you will find the question already present, awaiting your attention. This could be a question you face, a challenge you are experiencing, or a more searching inquiry about your life's direction.

Now, consider each potential response to the question, one by one, and listen. Listening in this context extends beyond the sensation of hearing; it involves a readiness to receive. This form of listening transcends the mind's incessant chatter, engaging the entirety of your being.

This skill sharpens over time, much like a musician discerning subtle nuances in sound. At first, your mind may wander, or you might feel unsure of what you are listening for. This is natural. Gently guide your attention back to your center and persist.

We cannot compel a response or summon it at will; our role is to create the conditions for an answer to emerge. Consider it as preparing a welcoming space for wisdom to appear rather than trying to force it into being.

The answer may manifest in various forms. Sometimes, it may come as a subtle feeling, a physical sensation, or a sudden insight that illuminates the way forward. At other times, it may reveal itself gradually, like a flower slowly opening. But we cannot force it to bloom before its time. Instead, we must foster an atmosphere of openness and attentiveness, allowing wisdom to emerge naturally. These insights often differ from regular thoughts, carrying a sense of certainty or rightness that sets them apart.

Be prepared to receive insights that may take time to make logical sense. The voice of wisdom often speaks in ways that transcend our usual patterns of thought. For instance, you might feel a strong urge to reach out to an old friend, only to discover later that they needed support at that exact moment. When such inclinations arise, note them and take them seriously, even when their purpose is not yet apparent; their meaning often becomes evident only in time.

If no immediate response arises, do not be discouraged. Keep going. The very act of posing the question clears your mind, creating a tranquil space where the right response can eventually surface in its own time and in its own way. With each attentive pause, your capacity to hear the voice of wisdom grows stronger. What begins as a faint impression may eventually become more recognizable. What once felt difficult becomes more familiar. You may find yourself pausing naturally throughout the day, bringing this form of listening into your routine interactions and decisions.

Whatever follows, trust this process. The answers you seek reside within, ready to be heard.

4. Try This

Dedicate the next few moments, even a few breaths, to reconnecting with your body and rediscovering your center. Begin by noticing the points where your body contacts the surface beneath you. Sense its weight pressing down, grounding you in the present. Set an intention for this exercise, whether to find calm, attend to your inner wisdom, or simply remain present.

Inhale. Hold as you count to seven (or for as long as comfortable). **Slowly exhale**.

With each breath, invite the muscles in your face to release any tension.

Inhale. Hold for a count of seven. **Slowly exhale**.

Allow the tension in your shoulders to ease.

Inhale. Hold for a count of seven. **Slowly exhale**.

Gently allow your chest muscles to relax and soften.

Inhale. Hold for a count of seven. **Slowly exhale**.

Repeat this cycle, inviting relaxation to move gradually down from the crown of your head to the tips of your toes. Bring your attention to your breath. Notice the air entering through your nostrils, feel your ribs expand and contract, and observe the gentle rise and fall of your abdomen. Resist the urge to hurry. Take the time as you need.

As thoughts arise, acknowledge them without attachment, then gently redirect your attention back to the breath. As your awareness settles, gradually direct it to the center of your being, perhaps near your heart, where you feel the movement of breath, or deeper within your abdomen. Visualize entering an inner sanctuary, a place of peace and tranquility.

While remaining centered here, notice any sensations within your body. It is continually communicating, offering insights into your emotions, desires, and inclinations. Draw in one final, unhurried breath. As you exhale, observe whether anything has shifted in your body or mind. What, if anything, has changed?

This brief exercise draws your attention inward. With regular practice, returning to this centered state becomes increasingly effortless, strengthening your ability to recognize and follow this inner guidance.

Our Bodies, Hearts, and Minds Confirm Its Truth

We often divide our experiences into physical, emotional, and mental categories. Yet these divisions are artificial, like the lines drawn on a map. These distinctions exist only in our perception, akin to political borders that do not alter the underlying landscape. When the voice of wisdom offers an answer, the alignment of our body, heart, and mind affirms its truth.

The body, grounded in the present, communicates our environment and internal state through physical sensations. The heart connects us to others, enabling us to understand different perspectives and recognize our interconnectedness. The mind projects into the future, analyzing potential outcomes, weighing options, and applying past learnings to new situations. Each offers vital clues.

Imagine you are considering a job offer. Your mind evaluates the salary, benefits, and career prospects. Your heart gauges your enthusiasm for the role and its alignment with your intentions. Meanwhile, your body registers enthusiasm or apprehension as you picture yourself in the new workspace. When these align — the offer makes sense logically, fulfills you emotionally, and brings physical calm — you recognize you have found the correct choice.

When alignment falters, a murmur of dissatisfaction takes its place. At times it is faint, at other times undeniable. It may appear as weariness, unease, or confusion. This discontent offers its own message, reminding us that something vital has been ignored. It is more than a warning; it is a sign to pause, a call to look again. Which part of our intelligence have we ignored?

Too often, we focus on treating symptoms rather than seeking to understand what they are pointing toward. We treat a tension headache with pain relievers instead of examining the suppressed anger or lingering anxiety at its root. We counter fatigue with caffeine rather than addressing sleep, stress, or emotional depletion. In relationships, we push aside discontent, making polite adjustments while avoiding harder conversations about misaligned expectations. We may even rationalize lingering doubts about a decision rather than examine what they are asking of us. When we focus only on symptoms, we risk overlooking the meaningful messages our body, heart, and mind seek to convey.

Recognizing the intelligence of our integrated self is vital to overall well-being. By attending to subtle signals, we gain the chance to identify underlying issues and address them at their source. This awareness supports more lasting and meaningful improvement.

When contemplating a decision, plausible answers may initially seem shrouded in uncertainty. Yet, with patience and receptivity, the right answer will reveal itself, like sunlight spreading across a forest. As this light of recognition dawns, your body responds in kind. You might notice your shoulders, once tense, easing downward. The tightness in your face and jaw may dissipate. Perhaps you feel an invisible band constricting your chest loosen its grip, allowing your lungs to expand with a full, satisfying breath. Some people experience a gentle tingling across their skin or a wave of energy surging through them. Warmth might blossom in your chest, spreading outward. Without conscious thought, the corners of your mouth may lift into a smile, or your head might nod in quiet affirmation. These physical responses vary from person to person, yet they all speak the language of revelation, your body's way of saying, *Yes, that is it.*

Your heart speaks the language of certainty. You notice the subtle quickening of your pulse, a surge that settles into a strong, steady rhythm. A focused warmth emerges from your core, radiating outward as your chest expands to accommodate this new understanding. As this warmth envelops you, you recognize a heightened sense of connection, not just to yourself but to others in your life. Yet this insight reaches beyond your personal sphere, touching lives you may never meet. From this connection springs a complex emotional response: perhaps a burst of purposeful energy, a flash of insight, or an unwavering determination. These feelings are balanced by a grounding calm that dissolves lingering doubts. As these sensations mingle and settle, they crystallize into firm confidence. It is a conviction acknowledging, *Yes, this path may have its challenges, and it is the right thing to do.*

Of course, each of us is different. The sensations that arise may vary with the nature of the decision or the surrounding context. You might experience this harmony when selecting a nourishing meal, with your body responding with immediate appreciation. When choosing the ideal gift for a loved one, your heart may swell with joy, anticipating their happiness. Contemplating a new venture, you could sense a sudden calm, your pulse steadying as a clear vision of success materializes.

Understanding your unique patterns and recognizing how alignment manifests is invaluable. Picture yourself as an artist blending colors on a palette. With each turn of the brush, you might feel a surge of energy, your emotions lift, and your imagination ignite. As you apply paint to canvas, every gesture brings the composition into perfect harmony, creating a masterpiece through each stroke.

Finding Your Center
Establishing a method for finding your center is an inherently personal process. As you begin, set aside time in a quiet place — perhaps a corner of your home, a peaceful outdoor spot, or wherever you reliably find tranquility. While it may be relatively easy to find calm in the comfort of your space, sustaining that centeredness amidst the unpredictability of everyday life is another matter. We seldom have the opportunity to retreat to our preferred sanctuaries before confronting important choices or challenges.

This reality underscores the importance of developing reliable practices that enable us to swiftly recenter ourselves, regardless of our circumstances. Simple habits like mindful breathing, counting to ten, focusing on a personal touchstone, or performing a quick body scan are effective techniques. Such practices, when employed regularly, serve as a gateway to finding your center and reconnecting with the wisdom within.

During my years as a practicing lawyer, I developed a unique habit that proved instrumental both in and out of the courtroom. I was an avid notetaker but not just on any paper. I used crisp, white notepads made of ninety-gram paper stock, never the flimsy tablets from the local office supply or the traditional yellow ones. The quality and feel invited hand to paper and thought to ink. But the real secret lay hidden at the end of each notepad. Tucked between the final page and the cardboard backing, I kept a photograph of my loyal companion Peaches, a border collie whom I affectionally called Superdog.

In high-stakes moments — whether in a trial, a contentious meeting, or a public speaking appearance — I would discreetly flip to the end of my notepad to catch a glimpse of that photo, her eyes gazing back at me openly and contentedly. That image of Superdog became an instant anchor, grounding me in the present and reminding me of what truly mattered. My shallow breathing would suddenly become fuller, my focus sharpening and tension falling away as I recalled playing together, the warmth of her leaping into my lap for a hug, or her faithful comforting presence. That simple act of remembering helped me reconnect with the center of my being, enabling me to approach whatever lay ahead with greater composure.

What started as a simple calming technique gradually evolved into something more purposeful. Initially, I would glance at the photo only during moments of high stress. Over time, I began to return to this practice in quieter moments, using it to reflect and make decisions. This technique transitioned from a stress reliever to a tool for calm reflection and informed decision-making. By disposition or professional demands, I often spent most of my time in my head, analyzing and reasoning. Thoughts of Superdog guided me back to the center of my being. Setting aside moments of quiet to concentrate on her and our time together served as a portal, transporting me closer to the center of my being. This practice enabled me to act with both logic and compassion, balancing the analytical demands of my profession with empathy and consideration for others.

Perhaps you have a similar memento, memory, or practice that serves as a gateway to inner peace or an aspect of your being that you might otherwise ignore: the thought of a loved one, a token, a picture, a memory of a place, or other cherished recollection. Consider focusing on your personal totem during moments of calm to reconnect with the associated feelings and sensations. With time, even a brief reflection on this memento can help you regain your center during stressful situations or when making important decisions.

Clarity, Lightness, and Purposefulness

Perhaps without realizing it, these small acts of centering do more than restore calm; they reconnect us with the stillness within. In returning to this space again and again, we experience a steadily growing sense of *clarity, lightness, and purposefulness*. Clarity cuts through the noise of the day, reads the quiet currents of cause and effect, and illuminates the best course of action. We grasp life's brevity and begin to move with clear intention. Freed from the needless struggle against reality and unburdened by what does not serve us, we feel lighter. We are lighter, buoyed by a newfound ease. As clarity and lightness take hold, purposefulness emerges — a steady force that provides direction and the resolve to follow through.

Our bodies awaken with energy, and our hearts open to connection. Even the simplest acts — preparing a meal, traveling from one place to another — acquire a renewed significance as we recognize their place within a greater whole. The awareness of a larger purpose steadies us, keeping the greater *why* in focus and sustaining our drive to move forward.

An athlete might realize that true success is not measured by the points they score but by how they elevate the team. A musician might recognize that music is not merely the faithful reproduction of notes but a conduit for expression. An executive might understand that effectiveness is not about working the longest hours but about dedicating time where it offers the greatest significance. A teacher might come to see that their role extends beyond imparting knowledge to awakening curiosity and inspiring the minds of the next generation. Each realization alters not only what a person does but also how they move through the world.

In our daily lives, these shifts heighten our appreciation for the environment around us. Each sunrise holds greater promise, every shared laugh echoes with warmth, and each act of kindness leaves an imprint beyond itself. We begin to shed unnecessary burdens, opening our eyes to the beauty, truth, and goodness within ourselves and our surroundings.

Ultimately, clarity, lightness, and purposefulness embolden us to act with confidence. We no longer merely exist; we live in greater harmony with ourselves and our community. This way of living mirrors the rhythms of nature. Just as a tree sheds its leaves in autumn to conserve energy for the seasons ahead, we release what no longer serves us. In doing so, we create space for new insights and experiences, adding understanding of ourselves and the world around us.

Summary

Chapter 7, "Engage the Voice of Wisdom," centers on turning inward to reconnect with the wisdom within, a confluence of knowledge, experience, and insight. This wisdom does not reject analysis or intuition; it integrates them. By learning to pause, return to one's center, and listen, you create the conditions in which this guidance can be received. When engaged, it speaks through body, heart, and mind, bringing them into agreement when a choice is sound and signaling caution when something has been missed. Ignoring this guidance often leads to dissatisfaction. Attending to it supports decisions that, over time, carry us toward the life we seek. As you reflect on this chapter, consider the following questions:

1. How do you distinguish what is right from what is wrong?
2. How does that inner knowing register in your body, heart, and mind?
3. Think of a decision in which all three were in agreement. What followed from that choice?
4. Recall a decision marked by hesitation or internal conflict. What followed from that choice?
5. What is one small step you can take to listen more closely to the wisdom within you?

Challenges

Self-Discovery: Set aside a few uninterrupted minutes to reflect on a time when you felt fully aligned with your inner wisdom. Begin with several slow breaths. Recall what you noticed physically, emotionally, and mentally at the moment of choice. Write briefly about how this sense of alignment influenced your action and what followed. Identify one signal that helped you recognize this inner guidance at the time.

Further Exploration: Speak with someone you trust about how they recognize inner guidance when making decisions. Invite them to describe the signals they notice and what helps them attend to those signals when life feels demanding. Afterward, write down one practice they described that you are willing to try.

Chapter 8 — Act

We must walk consciously only part way toward our goal,
and then leap in the dark to our success.
—Henry David Thoreau[34]

There are moments in life when you find yourself at the crossroads of significant change, fully conscious that the time to move forward is now. There is no turning back. The question is no longer about awareness; it is about readiness. Are you prepared to act?

To act is to breathe life into an intention. It is the bridge between thought and reality, to seize the moment when potential crystallizes into tangible change. Sometimes, it requires a bold step forward, a declaration of conviction. Other times, it manifests as the quiet strength of restraint, the deliberate choice of silence in a heated debate, where wisdom speaks louder than words.

Our lives consist of countless choices, each a moment that compels us to act. Yet how often does knowledge remain unrealized in the absence of action? We hesitate, suspended in the delicate balance between understanding and action. The unknown looms vast, both thrilling and terrifying.

But here is the truth: Once you know, you know. Each day of inaction is an act of self-betrayal, a squandered opportunity. Every day spent in conflict with your truth is a day that falls short of its potential. While doubts may linger, and they often do, action is the remedy. In doing, we dispel fears, restore integrity, and move closer to feeling alive. Rarely do we look back and wish we had delayed change. Instead, we regret the time lost, the days of our lives unlived.

As you reflect on your life today, consider where you need to make a change. How is your physical and mental well-being? Are your relationships nourishing and supportive? Does your work reflect your intentions and aspirations? If any aspect of your life fails to meet your true desires, remember: The power to transform it lies within you, regardless of how daunting it may appear.

Personal Account: Part Six

The way forward was clear: I needed to change careers. The question was no longer if but when. I knew my decision would alter the lives of those around me who had not sought these changes. How would they respond?

At this point, George, my law partner, was still in the dark. Over a decade of work together, we had developed a complementary partnership, understanding each other's strengths and weaknesses.

George was tall and lean with a thick head of jet-black hair. His experience as a military pilot sharpened his commanding presence. At his best, he was brilliant and charming. In the courtroom, he embodied the role of *everyman made good*, dismantling even formidable expert witnesses with a Tennessee drawl that sounded like honey poured from the barrel of a shotgun. Jurors adored him.

What George and I had in common were strict, military-trained fathers who instilled in us relentless drives to prove our worth, and a distinct type of anger. George externalized his anger, while I internalized mine. We both relished representing clients whom we perceived as disadvantaged, especially when pitted against larger, more established law firms. George coined our firm's unofficial motto: "The enemy has us outnumbered and surrounded on all sides; we can shoot in every direction. Our victory is assured."[35]

While we disagreed from time to time, our firm's proverbial guns were aimed outward, not at each other. We respected and trusted one another, deferring to each other's expertise. Over time, we divided our roles, George focusing on strategy and me on the firm's management. We also fell into a routine that fortified our bond. At the end of each day, as phone calls subsided and the staff began to trickle out, he would wander into my office and plop down on my couch, where we casually discussed topics from courthouse gossip to pending cases.

As I considered leaving the firm, something in me shifted. George sensed it even before I did. Though we had not discussed it, this change in my demeanor must have unsettled him. George's initial response to fear was anger. The day I informed him of my decision, he lashed out, accusing me of being foolish and throwing away my career. Any rational discussion quickly deteriorated, and he became increasingly aggressive in the days that followed.

During this period, I consulted with Phil. After relaying George's reaction, Phil offered transformative advice: "The path forward is through." The best way to approach George was not to avoid him but to confront him on his terms. A few days later, an opportunity arose.

It was a Thursday. George stormed into my office in a righteous fury, ostensibly over a line item in our monthly financial statement. Eyes narrowed, voice rising, finger jabbing at the page, he launched his tirade. Though I managed the firm's finances, he seemed more interested in attacking my management than clarifying the report. It was clear George wanted everyone to hear the dispute; he was spoiling for a fight.

For the first few minutes, I remained behind my desk, attempting to explain the numbers calmly. But as George's voice escalated, I took a calculated risk. Emboldened by Phil's words, I stood up, stepped toward George, and asserted that he was mistaken, my voice strong and resolute.

The argument escalated, our voices rising, faces turning crimson. Accusations and counteraccusations flew until we neared physical confrontation. In that moment, George bet $1,000 that I could not reconcile the disputed number in the report with the underlying data. Without hesitation, I accepted.

Wheeling around to my computer, George followed and stood behind me, barking commands. Ignoring the distraction, I opened the report. As the data appeared on the screen, I pointed out how the numbers perfectly aligned, proving my point.

George's face contorted with anger and resignation. "Fine, you want out? Then I want out," he erupted. "It is all yours. I am giving you the keys, and it will be your responsibility. Good luck." Then he stormed out, vanishing down the hall.

I stood motionless as the weight of the moment settled. The office was unnaturally still, silent except for the hum of the air-conditioning and the distant murmur of voices. I had won the argument, but the significance of what transpired was just becoming clear. George's abrupt departure and his final words permanently altered our relationship and the firm's future. Winning the war was now about more than just the firm. It encompassed the battle within me, an irrevocable commitment to change. I stood there, knowing the challenges ahead would be considerable and the real test of my resolve was yet to come.

We did not speak for days. Then, one evening, George reappeared in my office and sat on the couch, resuming an old habit. He thought I was leaving to start or join another practice and questioned my decision. I clarified I had no such plans. Though he still questioned my choice, he expressed his willingness to work things out. We did, not immediately but over the following weeks. In the months that followed, confrontations became rare, and our conversations grew more civil and productive. We resolved our differences amicably and dissolved our partnership on reasonable terms.

Overcoming the Resistance Within

Imagine a life where each day is a mirror image of the last, offering no variation or surprise. You wake at the same hour, in the same bed, beside the same person. Your routine remains unaltered: You consume identical meals, perform the same work, and engage in the same conversations. As you drift off to sleep, you know with certainty that tomorrow will be an exact copy of today, save for the fact that you will age by one day.

This thought exercise, which I revisit periodically, conjures an image of absolute stasis, an existence where nothing ever changes. Relationships neither strengthen nor fade. Your career stands motionless, neither advancing nor retreating. Your knowledge and abilities plateau, neither improving nor declining. The environment around you remains frozen, offering no novel experiences, surprises, or challenges. Conversations revolve around a fixed set of topics: weather, family, local gossip, sports, and the news story of the day. Every decision you have ever made remains unaltered.

Now consider: If given a month, or even a year, to reflect on this unchanging pattern, would you choose to sustain your current life, or would you seize the chance to alter its course?

We often acknowledge the need for change, yet knowing what we want or need is only the beginning. Acting on that knowledge is an entirely different challenge. Consider the well-established science behind a healthy life: eat nutritious foods, stay well hydrated, engage in both cardiovascular and strength training, get adequate sleep, reduce stress, and avoid harmful habits. This information is widely known, yet its implementation often proves daunting. We consume processed food, neglect exercise, compromise sleep, or revert to harmful behaviors — again.

Why does this disconnect between knowledge and action persist?

While external influences like societal expectations and financial constraints undoubtedly play a role, the most formidable barrier to a fulfilling life often lies within. The familiar feels more comfortable, safer, and less demanding than initiating change. Procrastination, fear, and self-doubt work in concert to preserve established patterns. When these prove inadequate, our minds craft compelling justifications and elaborate narratives designed to uphold the status quo, even when it no longer serves our best interests.

We may convince ourselves that tomorrow will present fewer challenges, that we will find more time or more energy, or experience a sudden surge of determination. Or perhaps we cling to the faint hope that our difficulties will simply dissipate on their own.

These rationalizations, while comforting, merely delay the inevitable confrontation with change. The truth is that change is inherently discomfiting. It disrupts our established routines, challenges our assumptions, and compels us to confront aspects of ourselves we might prefer to leave unexamined. Meanwhile, the days of our lives beat relentlessly forward.

To create a different tomorrow, we must confront our internal resistance and commit to meaningful change. This often demands uncomfortable actions such as reconsidering firmly held beliefs, initiating challenging conversations, taking a stand, or forging new directions. More daunting still, it may require acknowledging our failures, offering sincere amends, or relinquishing control. These moments ask more of us than effort alone. They ask for honesty.

Rather than meeting this call directly, we often turn away. Instead of looking inward to ask the difficult questions, we remain in motion. We work relentlessly in pursuit of recognition or added responsibility. We fill our days accumulating possessions and experiences. All the while, we tell ourselves that forward motion, regardless of direction, is preferable to stopping and risking being left behind.

And yet, truth has a way of persisting. At the center of our being lies an awareness, a knowing of what we are capable of and what we truly want. It does not demand attention or force itself into view. Still, it holds, informed by memory, values, and lived experience, even as we attempt to suppress it.

Living at odds with this inner knowing creates dissonance, an unsettling tension that reverberates throughout our entire being. It appears in familiar forms: paralytic overthinking that delays decisions, chronic procrastination that stalls action, or debilitating fear that inflates the perceived cost of change. These patterns are not failures of discipline or effort. They are signals, pointing us back toward what we already recognize but have not yet allowed ourselves to face.

Paradoxically, a more vibrant, fulfilling, and successful existence often requires a counterintuitive response. Rather than accelerating, we pause. Rather than outrunning what we sense, we turn inward and listen with honesty. Overcoming the resistance within does not begin with force or exertion, but with a willingness to stop, acknowledge what we know, and allow that recognition to guide what comes next.

These actions have the power to transform our lives. Yet with each moment of hesitation, the future we envision becomes more distant.

Each day of inaction widens the gap between our present reality and the life we aspire to lead. The time to act is now. We stand at a clear crossroads: disregard our inner truth and accept the consequences, or summon the courage to act. Our future selves depend on the choices we make today.

The Power of Why

Breaking free from self-imposed limitations requires honest self-inquiry. At the heart of this process lies a powerful tool: the simple question *Why?*

Consider this scenario: You are a working professional with a demanding career, juggling family responsibilities and a packed social calendar. Your reputation for reliability is a source of pride. You work long hours, often sacrificing time with your family and friends. Meanwhile, a disquieting sense of unfulfillment takes root. Your body aches under the weight of persistent stress. Sleep is elusive as your mind races through endless lists of tasks. Joy feels distant, replaced by a sense of exhaustion and disconnection.

Now ask yourself why.

Why do you work long hours? Because I need to advance my career. Why do you need to advance your career? Because I want financial security. Why do you want financial security? Because I fear instability. Why do you fear instability? Because I experienced economic hardship as a child.

Through this process, you might discover that your relentless pursuit of success stems not from genuine passion but from a fear of inadequacy or a craving for external validation. Or perhaps you consistently prioritize others' needs over yours, avoid difficult conversations, or struggle to set boundaries. These behaviors might stem from unconscious motivations: a need for security, a fear of judgment, a desire for approval, or anxiety about making the wrong choice. By repeatedly asking *why*, we can uncover the unconscious motivations that influence the choices we make, choices that often determine the course of our lives.

One incredibly successful entrepreneur went through this exercise and found that, despite his company's continued success over decades, he felt an increasing sense of unease. Through self-inquiry, he discovered a long-repressed fear of being seen as inadequate due to his education at a small public college, particularly as compared to employees with degrees from prestigious universities. This fear, stemming from a decision made at age seventeen, continues to drive his behavior today, affecting his ability to delegate and trust his team.

Asking *why* goes beyond surface-level introspection. It is a form of self-inquiry that requires the courage to face uncomfortable truths, as well as the patience to endure uncertainty. This process is fundamentally different from casual self-reflection; it demands pushing past our initial responses to uncover the true motivations behind our actions and beliefs.

As unconscious beliefs and patterns come to light, label them. You might identify the fear of financial dependence, the fear of not being wanted, or the fear of not being good enough. Naming these patterns distances you from them, allowing for a more objective evaluation of how they influence your life. You might notice how fear of inadequacy drives you to overwork or how a need for approval sabotages your relationships. This powerful recognition allows you to see the invisible forces that have guided your decisions.

This is where the voice of wisdom proves invaluable. As you make choices, pause to ask yourself: *How is this decision influenced by the beliefs I have uncovered?* This simple question can help you distinguish between actions driven by old fears and those aligned with your current intentions.

Our most repressed fears frequently stand between us and the realization of our full potential. As the entrepreneur's story reminds us, the fear of looking bad often prevents us from being great; by courageously asking *why* and confronting these fears, we open ourselves to new possibilities.

Overcoming the Expectations of Others

After confronting our internal barriers and clarifying our direction, we encounter a new set of challenges: external influences. These range from our immediate circle of family and friends to people we work with, those we encounter socially, and even public figures we admire from afar. Well-meaning advice from loved ones, societal norms reinforced by our communities, workplace expectations, and the ideals promoted by influential personalities all exert pressure on our choices and self-perception.

Our social existence is intrinsically complex, governed by roles determined by our family, socioeconomic status, and cultural background. Educational systems, religious organizations, and governmental bodies all create and enforce certain standards of behavior and achievement. As we mature, we internalize these expectations, which influence our identities and perceptions in subtle yet significant ways. For example, a child born into a family of doctors might feel pressured to pursue medicine, not only by her parents but also by her teachers and community. Similarly, someone raised in a religious community might find their personal aspirations guided by both family traditions and the broader expectations of their faith institution.

We all face habitual expectations from those around us. Imagine a typical day: A colleague suggests you should not outshine your peers. Your friends insist you join them for social activities, even when you would rather focus on your interests. Society presents images of how you *should* look, act, and live. These voices, overt and subtle, form a chorus that can drown out your inner wisdom.

The power of these *shoulds* lies in their familiarity and the discomfort of defying them. When you choose to prioritize your individual aspirations over societal norms by pursuing an unconventional career path, you are not merely making a personal choice — you are challenging the habits and perhaps the insecurities of those around you. Their resistance is not about your decision; it is a reflection of their choices.

This resistance to breaking free from the *shoulds* stems from ingrained psychological mechanisms. We are inherently social creatures, wired to seek approval and avoid ostracism. Our minds often perceive social disapproval as a threat, triggering stress responses that make defying expectations physically and emotionally uncomfortable. Moreover, we tend to internalize the expectations of others, particularly those we respect or love. The external *you should* gradually transforms into an internal *I should* or even *I am not good enough because I did not*.

In our increasingly interconnected world, constant exposure to others' lives and achievements amplifies the chorus of external voices. This barrage of information can fuel an endless cycle of comparison, where we measure ourselves against an idealized version of our potential or the curated highlights of others' lives.

Yet societal expectations and their accompanying *shoulds* are not immutable. They evolve over time through individuals who dare to reimagine or challenge the status quo and question conventional wisdom. Consider Aristotle, a revered philosopher who embodied the accepted definition of wisdom in his time. He concluded that the Sun rotates around the Earth based on how it appears to us. Combining his belief in a God-centered universe with his observations, he constructed the following syllogism: God created the world (Earth) as the center of the universe; we observe the Sun rise in the east and set in the west; therefore, the Sun orbits the Earth.

While this belief seems fundamentally flawed today, it was the accepted truth for nearly two thousand years until Galileo and his telescope shifted our understanding of celestial bodies. Aristotle's reasoning exemplified the conventional wisdom of the time, a belief generally accepted as true, which may no longer be valid or was never true.

This example illustrates how conventional wisdom, often the product of past experiences or traditions, may not suit our current circumstances. It is wise to routinely question these long-held beliefs to ensure they still serve us in the present.

We are continuously evolving. You are not the same person you were a decade ago, a year ago, or even yesterday. Your beliefs and perspectives shift, echoing the ancient wisdom that "everything is in motion." How can we protect ourselves against the fallibility of conventional wisdom and the inevitability of change? The answer lies in habitually questioning *What is true now?* This approach allows us to stay open to new knowledge, evolve, adapt, and approach a clearer understanding of our reality.

Only by looking beyond it can we align our actions with our true intentions and aspirations. As we envision the future, we must consider the decisions required today to bring it into being. Let the knowledge of the past inform us but not confine us. This approach leads to a life unburdened by regret, defined by choices that reflect our values.

At various points in our lives, we all arrive at crossroads where societal expectations and inner wisdom diverge. Recognizing the right direction is only the first step. The real challenge lies in mustering the courage to act on this knowledge, especially when it contradicts external expectations. This requires discernment between external pressures and authentic desires, as well as the fortitude to stand by our decisions.

Acting on inner wisdom does not guarantee easy decisions or immediate clarity; it often involves facing uncertainty, questioning long-held beliefs, and making choices that challenge societal definitions of success. This process can be uncomfortable, as it may mean departing from the well-trodden path and redefining personal measures of achievement. Yet this discomfort often signals progress. By consistently acting on our inner voice, we develop a stronger sense of self and become more adept at making and implementing decisions that truly serve us.

The objective is not to ignore external influences but to rather to establish meaningful dialogue between the wisdom within us and the environment around us. This balance enables us to draw from the collective knowledge of the past while staying true to what is right in the present.

The Next Step in the Process

Returning to my story, I had reached a certain level of success as an established lawyer. I had amassed a wealth of experience, built a successful firm, attracted intriguing clients, and fulfilled my aspiration of helping others. Yet, despite these outward achievements, a persistent disquiet lingered within me, whispering that something essential was missing. The fleeting nature of life echoed in my mind, urging me to live each moment meaningfully and seek out my true path.

One day, I finally summoned the courage to confront this nagging thought. The question was daunting: Should I continue practicing law or pursue a new career in business? As I searched for the answer, a clear, resonant voice emerged from within me. It did not speak a single word or phrase; instead, it revealed a vision of applying my skills in a new arena.

Venturing into finance involved tremendous risk. It meant starting over, relinquishing a reliable salary for more than a year, and accepting the probability of failure. Moreover, my identity as a lawyer, the final arbiter of what action to take, would be irrevocably altered. I had always been the one clients turned to for the final word when they needed to make decisions in the courtroom, for their businesses, or for their lives. In finance, I would be just one among many voices.

My peers, successful lawyers who had consistently followed the traditional track, were vocal in their skepticism. Their questions and doubts mirrored my internal reservations. Yet I chose to view these voices as challenges to overcome rather than deterrents. How could I, alone among them, dare to diverge? The external voices of resistance echoed alongside my internal reservations — each with a label, such as *fear of failure*, *fear of uncertainty*, and *identity crisis*. However, I recognized these voices for what they were: signs of resistance.

Amidst these voices, I found my sanctuary and inspiration in the most unexpected corners. Two mementos reminded me of the choices ahead. One was a note from a fortune cookie taped to my refrigerator that read, "It is better to attempt something noble and fail than to never try at all." The other was a baseball card featuring Michael Jordan, which I affixed to the refrigerator alongside the fortune cookie message. Every day, I would look at that card and ask myself how long I would keep deviating from my purpose, just as Jordan had when he stepped away from the NBA, in the prime of his basketball career, to pursue his dream of playing baseball.

Today, the outcome of that decision is unmistakable. In my current work, I have influenced more people than I ever could have as a lawyer. The transition, particularly in the early years, came with its share of challenges and missteps, and it was far from easy. Yet each experience pushed me to evolve in ways that remaining in the safety of my law practice never would have. Over time, the vague intentions I had when entering law sharpened into a clearer sense of purpose. I chose to live without regret, to heed the call of wisdom, and to pursue a career more aligned with my true aspirations. By facing discomfort and trusting that inner voice, I began forging a life uniquely my own.

Summary

Chapter 8, "Act," examines the resistance that often arises between knowing what to do and doing it. Internal hesitation and external expectations operate as countervailing influences on action. Here, acting does not always require visible or dramatic change. It may take the form of restraint, initiating a difficult conversation, or questioning accepted norms. In most situations, action begets some degree of uncertainty. When action follows inner knowing, intention and behavior begin to align. When action is deferred, unresolved questions persist and the range of viable responses gradually narrows. As you reflect on this chapter, consider the following questions:

1. What expectations from family, work, or society influence how you behave?

2. Where do you notice a gap between knowing what to do and acting on that knowledge?

3. What would need to change for your actions to more consistently reflect what you know to be right?

4. Where might restraint be the appropriate form of action?

5. What tends to follow when action is delayed or avoided?

Challenges

Self-Discovery: Recall a time when you acted in alignment with your inner knowing, despite fear or doubt. Write briefly about what allowed you to proceed, how it felt to take action, and what became clear only afterward. Then turn to the present. Identify one area of your life where action has been postponed. Name one specific step that would move you out of delay and into motion.

Further Exploration: Speak with one person whose judgment you respect. Ask them to describe situations in which they know what needs to be done yet hesitate to act. Invite them to reflect on what typically holds them back, whether internal, external, or situational, and what ultimately moves them to proceed. Then consider which of those same patterns you recognize in yourself and which of the strategies they described could help you move from knowing to acting in your own decisions.

Chapter 9 — Observe and Adapt

It is not the most intellectual of the species that survives;
it is not the strongest that survives; but the species that
survives is the one that is able best to adapt and adjust
to the changing environment in which it finds itself
—Leon C. Megginson[36]

The final stage of our process, observe and adapt, is not just a single action; it is an ongoing practice of learning and improvement, informed by both successes and failures. Decisions are not endpoints but waypoints along the continuum of life. Each of us is an accumulation of information, insights, and experiences that help us better understand how our actions can influence the future, provided we pay attention. This process begins by developing a heightened sense of self-awareness, observing our behavior in each moment while seeking to understand the underlying causes.

Do we pause to reflect in moments of choice? If so, what thoughts, beliefs, memories, emotions, or sensory information are influencing our decisions? By directing our attention inward, we uncover the unconscious and automatic influences that determine our responses. This awareness enables us to adjust before acting, granting us a more objective perspective and guiding us toward wiser action over time.

As we move from the immediacy of self-observation, these moment-to-moment insights extend beyond the present, offering a rich context for regular reflection. In this space of contemplation, we can identify recurring patterns and habits and address broader questions: Who am I? What do I seek in life? Do my decisions reflect my true desires, for my benefit and the benefit of those around me?

We change, the people around us change, and the environment around us remains in constant flux. Each new insight presents an opportunity to adapt. This leads to a fundamental question at the heart of our existence: As the world evolves and changes, how will you respond? Will you persist in your current way of being, or will you choose to adapt?

Personal Account: Part Seven

Having decided to transition into business, I reflected on what I had learned from my legal career and the decision-making process itself. Beyond the tangible skills of the law, three specific insights emerged.

First, the longer we ignore the dissonance between who we are and how we behave, the more we become strangers to ourselves. The first decade of practicing law held meaning for me. I worked with conviction and believed in the value of what I was doing. Over time, that conviction faded. Perhaps the anger had quieted, replaced by a confidence that no longer required proving. But I began to question what justice meant and whether it could be achieved through the work I was doing. I thought less about those I served and more about my own advancement. The law had not changed. I had. What once felt principled began to feel performative. I said what I was supposed to say but no longer believed it. I did what was expected but in ways I no longer admired. I saw this happening and did not correct it. I became an observer of my own conduct, increasingly estranged from the person I had once trusted myself to be.

Still, I stayed. Doubt and fear made postponement to an indefinite point in the future feel reasonable, even responsible. The decision did not fade; it pressed closer. Maybe next year became maybe next month, then maybe tomorrow, until delay itself became a pattern. With each passing day, I traded time for money and labeled it practicality, even as I grew further removed from the person I wanted to be. Only when I stopped negotiating and acknowledged the inconsistency between how I was living and what I knew to be true did action become possible. What followed was not ease but relief: a return to something more honest and a way of living that no longer required justification.

The second insight was this: the next era of our lives is often already present in the current one. Once I began to question my direction, I recognized the clues that had been there all along. I had always thought of myself as a lawyer. Even while running my own firm, I did not regard it as a business in itself. That perception shifted when I assumed responsibility for managing a healthcare facility. Managing people, interpreting data, and guiding an organization through uncertainty were not legal tasks. They were familiar forms of responsibility, already in use, and transferable to business. What I had imagined to be a departure was, in fact, a clearer view of what had already begun.

Leaving law brought an immediate sense of relief. At first, the change arrived as a dawning, sensed before it could be spoken. I felt lighter. In the days that followed, the work was no easier, yet the tension that had accompanied nearly every choice began to subside. This was not because I had assumed a new identity. It was because I had taken a step in a truer direction and remained attentive to what followed.

The third insight concerned the decision-making process itself. It is not a single act but a skill honed over time. For years, I waited for certainty, expecting the right moment to announce itself. What practice revealed instead was something else. Progress begins by asking the right question, then remaining attentive as the answer emerges.

I came to understand that sound decisions draw from three sources: the body, the heart, and the mind. Each contributes insight, yet none is sufficient on its own. The body offers signals conditioned by habit and experience, often helpful, yet sometimes mistaken. The heart can stir empathy and emotion, drawing us toward what feels good without regard for consequence. The mind can illuminate patterns and perceptions just as easily as it can rationalize or distort.

Anyone who has returned to the same demanding routine recognizes these signals. For a runner, any one or all three may arise on a given day. The mind offers temptation to remain in a warm bed. The heart suggests that today is not the day. Even after stepping outside, the body may protest with each stride, insisting the distance is too far. Yet if you stay with it, something begins to ease. Movement finds rhythm. Effort becomes coordinated in turn. When the run ends, body, heart, and mind converge, reveling in the accomplishment. This is the nature of internal signals. They change, day by day and sometimes step by step.

With practice, I learned how to listen. Not to a stronger or more convincing voice, but to something more consistent and more true. I sensed it near the center of my being. In that space, I could engage without inner conflict and act without judgment. Returning to that place became the discipline. Each decision offered an opportunity to examine both the choice itself and the manner of choosing. That, I came to understand, is the practice. We observe. We adjust. And through repetition, we learn to act with greater care.

Self-Observation and Self-Regulation

Imagine possessing a superpower that allows you to pause time, assess your thoughts and actions, and make real-time adjustments. This is the essence of self-observation. Self-observation, much like mindfulness, involves cultivating an awareness of your thoughts and actions. However, unlike mindfulness, self-observation seeks to uncover the *why* behind your choices. Understanding this distinction can transform how you move through life.

We are complex beings, often guided by motives we only faintly perceive. We react, decide, and speak without fully understanding what drives us. A sharp tone with someone we care for. A withdrawal from responsibility even as we know better. A surge of envy or defensiveness that arrives without invitation. We notice ourselves disengaging, rationalizing, avoiding, yet we do not stop. We hear the sharpness in our voice but do not soften it. Something in us recoils even as we continue. In these moments, the discomfort is immediate. We are not confused after the fact; we are aware mid-act, and that awareness lingers, not as guilt but as a slow erosion of self-respect, a sense that we have abandoned something we meant to hold. Without a way to interrupt this cycle, these small departures from ourselves accumulate. Like the subtle pull of ocean tides, they can carry us away from our intentions and desires, all while giving the illusion of choice. So how do we break free from these automatic responses? The answer begins with self-observation.

At its core, self-observation involves three important steps. First, notice what is happening now: Become an expert observer of yourself to ensure your behavior aligns with your intentions. Second, assess what actually happened: Did you achieve the intended results? Third, identify what you learned: Quickly reflect on why the results did or did not match your intentions.

This process is not about prolonged introspection; it is about making precise real-time adjustments. Picture a chef during dinner service, tasting a sauce and deciding in a split second to adjust with wine instead of lemon. His hand reaches for the bottle almost before his mind has processed why, the result of thousands of hours of cooking, tasting, and practice. This is the kind of acute awareness we are seeking, where observation, assessment, and adjustment flow together as one fluid motion.

Self-observation begins with becoming a keen observer of yourself, your environment, and the people around you. This objectivity helps you notice patterns and behaviors you might otherwise overlook.

Now, let us explore what happens in the moment. You may be engaged in a heated discussion with a family member about a sensitive topic — perhaps politics, spending habits, or why your brother always seems to shirk responsibility. Your relative makes a statement that ignites a strong emotional response within you.

Your initial impulse might be to respond defensively or lash out. Practicing self-observation gives you the ability to stop yourself before you react. Are you at your equilibrium, or do you feel off-balance? Consider physical factors: Are you hungry or tired? What about your emotional state? Do you feel connected to those around you or strangely distant? And what of your mind: Is it calm and focused, or racing with anxiety?

Setting Aside Time to Reflect

While self-observation helps us catch ourselves in the moment, reflection allows us to see where those moments lead — and what moves beneath them. It reveals not only the arc of our actions but the impulses that guide them. Over time, we begin to notice which instincts govern us, which patterns persist, and what our choices, taken together, suggest about how we are living and what we are living toward.

Reflection is easy to postpone, but it begins simply. Five minutes of honest attention can reveal more than we expect. Longer interludes may offer more, but there is no standard. Begin where you are. Use this time as a silent dialogue with yourself. You might start by reviewing the day: Where did I place my attention? Where was I my best self? What gave me energy, and what drew it away? Then turn outward: Who am I grateful for? Who might have needed my care, and did I offer it?

It is a practice of return: to equilibrium, to integrity, to what endures beneath the noise of daily distractions. In time, reflection becomes not only a habit but a stabilizing presence. It clears away the inessential, revealing something truer, a coherence between how you act and what matters most.

From that place of centeredness, a different quality of awareness emerges, alert to what so often slips past. From this more honest vantage, questions gather of their own accord: What draws me, what do I return to, and what remains unfinished? As we follow these threads, we begin to see that our goals are not just about achievement but about meaning. And meaning often lies beneath the goal itself, in the longing it expresses, the connection it promises, or the change it dares us to make.

We often strive for ambition and accomplishment, envisioning a life that offers lasting fulfillment. Whether it is becoming a general manager, planning a wedding in Hawaii, or hiking a thousand miles on the Appalachian Trail, these goals give us something specific to strive toward. But beyond these visible milestones lies something even more significant: the *why* behind the goal. This is the foundation of fulfillment. Ask yourself: Beyond the title of general manager, what do I truly desire? Is it mastery of your field or greater self-confidence? Is the Hawaiian wedding about strengthening your partnership, sharing joy with loved ones, or creating lasting memories? For the thousand-mile hike, are you seeking a connection with nature, testing your limits, or proving what you are truly capable of?

Our goals should evolve as we do to reflect who we are and what we want. Ask yourself: Do these goals still align with my intentions and aspirations? Does working toward them bring me joy, or am I sacrificing today for a better tomorrow? Am I creating meaningful memories along the way? Do these pursuits make me feel truly alive?

If your goals no longer fit, it is time to adjust. This may mean reexamining existing goals or setting entirely new ones. Progress is not about rigidly adhering to a plan but about adapting to the changes in your environment and who you are.

When our goals align with our true selves, we often experience inner peace. Our emotional responses stabilize, and we see ourselves more clearly. We become less preoccupied with narratives of judgment about ourselves and those around us. Instead, we offer warmth and compassion instinctively. The relentless compulsion of *more, faster* now softens as we become increasingly content with our lives. Most important, we dwell less on regrets from the past or anxieties about the future. Our appreciation of the present becomes stronger.

Actively Adapting

Think of the most interesting people you know. Are they not also, more often than not, the ones you would call *wise*? For good reason. Their lives rarely follow a single line. They change direction, not abruptly but with intention. A new city. A new role. A reimagining in how they live, relate, or think. Not because they were forced or their lives were broken. Not because they were restless but because they sensed it was the right time. They invited change that required something more of them. Rather, they invited what would require them to adapt. They acted and accepted what would follow.

Adaptation is not merely how we survive; it is a biological and social imperative for living well in a changing world. It is not simply a reaction to change but the deliberate development of foresight and flexibility, the foundation of resilience. As a species, we have endured by adjusting to threat. As individuals, we progress by responding to what we learn, both through our own experience and by observing the behavior and results of others. We begin by watching. We notice what has changed in our surroundings, in our relationships, or within ourselves. Then we reflect, reconsidering our assumptions and revising our responses to match the conditions we now face. Without adaptation, we fall into repetition. We mistake habit for direction, then allow those habits to harden into principles we no longer question.

You can see the need for adaptation in the arc of a life. As children, we begin with play, discovery, and a sense of wonder. These are not discarded but carried forward. In school, we learn to channel them into attention, discipline, and sustained effort. Later, we apply these habits to our work, where we are no longer measured by potential but by results. Some of us become partners, parents, or caretakers. Each role draws on what came before but also asks for something new. The challenge is not only what we must learn but what we must revise. What mattered at one stage may no longer hold. What once felt certain becomes more complex. With each season

— and sometimes each year, even each day — we are drawn back to the question: Who am I now, and how will I respond?

But knowing that change is constant does not mean we know how to meet it. Some patterns repeat with such regularity that we begin to assume the outcome will change on its own. But adaptation is not automatic. Like the acquisition of wisdom, it is not a function of time or experience. It depends on what we do with that time and what we learn from that experience. Reaction is not revision. Reaction protects. Adaptation inquires. Reaction resists. Adaptation learns. It asks us to notice what no longer works, to interpret what has changed, and to respond accordingly.

Anyone who has taken a statistics course has encountered the familiar riddle: If you flip a fair coin ninety-nine times and it lands heads each time, what is the chance of heads on the one-hundredth? Still 50 percent. It is obvious when we speak of coins. But what about when it is the same disagreement with your partner? The same avoidance of a task at work? The same conversation with your child that ends in silence? We often convince ourselves that something will be different even as nothing has changed in how we act. Just as we resist believing that each coin flip is independent, we resist believing that familiar circumstances still require us to choose anew.

Change can come suddenly: as a revelation or a disruption. An unexpected health event. The day your first child is born. A redrawing of responsibilities in your work. A conversation that unsettles something you thought was fixed. Or perhaps someone says something, simply and without intent, and it transforms how you see your relationship to a person, a place, or a past version of yourself. These moments arrive without warning, and yet they leave no doubt. You feel it immediately, not as a theory but as a turning.

More often, adaptation emerges gradually. A small correction repeated over time. A behavior once resisted becomes familiar. You commit to walking ten thousand steps each day. Not because the number matters but because it gets you outside. Your body begins to settle. Your thinking clears. Over time, the habit replaces what came before. It provides the structure that carries you from one version of yourself to the next. *What structures are you building now? And are they strong enough to support who you are becoming?* So when your physician recommends resistance training, it does not feel like a disruption. You already make time for movement. You already know how to adjust.

That process is not always easy. Some days, the walk is difficult. Some days, it rains. You hesitate. You want to skip it. Other days, you begin reluctantly and find rhythm halfway through. Occasionally, you surprise yourself. The task remains the same, but how you meet it does not. Your internal signals vary. And that, too, is information. Obstacles can be instruction. A setback can show you where the old habit still has a hold. You pay attention. You revise. You learn to recognize progress in smaller signs: the walk completed, the skipped step made up the next day, the moment of resistance followed by movement. You adjust again. And you keep going.

Adaptation is not a phase, and it is not an endpoint. It is not a break between periods of certainty. It is part of how we live — if our aim is to live well. Change will come. It always does. Circumstances evolve, then regress. Familiar patterns return under different names. The same questions resurface in unfamiliar forms. The question is not whether change will arrive. The question is whether we will meet it with resolve or wait until it decides for us. These are not theoretical questions. They come to each of us, again and again. And each time, we must decide whether to choose our destiny or be led into a story we hoped never to tell.

Summary

Chapter 9, "Observe and Adapt," reminds us that acting is not the final step. Each decision yields information about what drives us in the moment and what results follow. Through observing our behavior, we begin to recognize patterns, including recurring reactions, habits of avoidance, and familiar forms of self-justification. This awareness allows for real-time adjustments, both small and significant, before a reaction becomes action. Reflection afterward helps confirm what worked, what did not, and why. Because circumstances are continually changing, this ongoing attention matters. By observing and adapting, decisions become less reflexive and more responsive to what is actually occurring, both within us and around us. As you reflect on this chapter, consider the following questions:

1. How do physical or emotional states such as fatigue, hunger, or stress affect your decisions?

2. When you notice these states, how often do you adjust before acting?

3. In recent a situation, what did you do automatically, even though you later wished you had responded differently?

4. How often do you set aside time to consider the consequences of your actions?

5. Based on what you have observed, what is one small adjustment you could make going forward?

Challenges

Self-Discovery: Identify a recurring pattern in how you make decisions, such as overanalysis, reliance on instinct, or deferring to others. Recall one recent situation in which this pattern served you well and one in which it led to regret or limitation. What signals appeared afterward that revealed the difference? Based on what you observed, note one specific adjustment you would test the next time this pattern arises.

Further Exploration: Speak with someone you trust about a specific area of their life where they noticed their usual way of responding was no longer working. Ask what first signaled the need for change and what made it difficult to respond differently at the time. Then ask what they did instead. Afterward, note which of those signals or obstacles you recognize in yourself and what this conversation suggests about how you might respond differently going forward.

Chapter 10 — A Time to Practice

"You are fettered," said Scrooge, trembling. "Tell me why?"
"I wear the chain I forged in life," replied the Ghost. "I
made it link by link, and yard by yard, I girded it on my
own free will, and of my own free will I wore it."
—Charles Dickens[37]

Now that you have a solid grasp of the seven-step decision-making process, it is time to put this knowledge into practice. Each decision you make is an opportunity to strengthen your understanding of the steps and gain confidence in your ability to apply them. What better way to reinforce these skills?

Consider sailing between islands in the Mediterranean. Reading about sailing, taking lessons, or imagining the voyage may offer valuable insights. However, nothing can replace the experience of hoisting the sails, feeling the wind's pull, or adjusting your balance to the rush of water and the rhythmic rise and fall of the waves beneath you. Then, there is the sight of the vast blue sea that surrounds you, with distant islands scattered like jewels on the horizon.

Soon, you discover the difference between preparation and practice. The wind shifts. A current pulls you off course. Every moment demands decisive action. You adjust the sails, correct your course, and adapt to the sea's ever-changing conditions. Yet, with time and experience, you learn to read the waves, feel the boat's subtle movements, and anticipate changes in the weather.

Life is like that. Its unpredictability imbues it with vibrancy and excitement. Just as a seasoned sailor learns to steer through unfamiliar waters, mastering the art of decision-making requires consistent practice. We learn to read our surroundings and respond to change as it arises. Above all, it demands that we become improvisers with a wide imagination and steadfast determination.

Rather than drift aimlessly with the tides, are you ready to chart your course?

Start Now

Begin by pausing for a moment to recall a decision that has been weighing on your mind. Whether it is a long-standing dilemma, such as contemplating a career change; a more immediate challenge, like repairing a strained relationship; or even a seemingly simple choice, such as where to go on your next vacation, each decision holds the potential for meaningful reflection. Do not dismiss a decision because it seems trivial. If it stirs something within you, it deserves attention. Unresolved matters, personal or professional, linger in the mind, manifesting as persistent unease. This irresolution saps energy and focus, diverting attention from productive pursuits.

Once you have identified your decision, visualize it fully. What is at stake? Why does it trouble you? Picture the consequences of inaction and then imagine the relief of resolution. This examination naturally propels you toward action.

Next, write down the seven steps:

1. Ask the question.
2. Acknowledge your immediate response.
3. Seek perspective.
4. Envision someone wise.
5. Engage the voice of wisdom.
6. Act.
7. Observe and adapt.

Each step contains subparts, nuances to consider as you move through the process. For instance, when contemplating what a wise person might ask (step 4), consider what the older, wiser you might recommend. By familiarizing yourself with each of the steps and their subparts, you will be better prepared to approach the decision-making process effectively.

The act of writing serves dual purposes: It frames your decision-making process and promotes objectivity. Moreover, it often sparks fresh ideas, prompting you to consider the issue from new angles as you begin to see it from a new point of view.

Creating the Conditions for Success

To make the most of the process, set aside a brief, uninterrupted period to carefully consider each of the questions. Fifteen to twenty minutes is a good starting point. Naturally, the time required for a decision depends on its importance and context. Generally, the more significant the decision and its potential influence on your life, the more time you should allocate to the process. With practice, the process will go faster.

Be wary of slipping into the trap of overanalysis. Excessive deliberation often leads to paralysis, trapping you in an endless cycle of indecision. This stagnation can result in missed opportunities or, worse, leave circumstances to decide for you. The regret that follows is not for the choice you made but for the one you failed to make. Sometimes, deciding, even if imperfect, is better than making no decision at all.

Approach each question with unflinching honesty. This is perhaps the most difficult part of the process, as it requires genuine introspection and self-compassion. It can be tempting to deceive ourselves, but honesty about our thoughts, relationships, and past decisions is essential. Without it, we risk basing our choices on flawed foundations, and any expectation of a good decision becomes a delusion.

Finally, commit to seeing your decision through to completion. Chapter 8, "Act," reminds us that following through on decisions is just as important as making them. Without action, even the most well-considered decision remains merely a thought.

A Real-Life Illustration

While earlier chapters explored how the decision-making process applied to my professional life, this story shifts to something far more personal, a decision that lingered in my mind for years: whether to reconcile with my estranged father, whom I had not spoken to in sixteen years, more than half my adult life.

If you have ever been entangled in a strained relationship with a family member, friend, or colleague, you understand the far-reaching effects: an undercurrent of unease, sudden surges of anger or sadness at the slightest reminder, or persistent curiosity about their life. You may attempt to dismiss these feelings, but they inevitably resurface, leaving you in a state of unresolved tension.

Disentangling yourself from these emotions is difficult and can exact a heavy toll on your emotional well-being, gradually coloring your interactions and eroding your sense of peace.

In my case, the estrangement between my father, Edmund, and me was not rooted in the typical reasons that divide many families, such as addiction, violence, or physical distance. Despite living close by, our separation was a deliberate choice. I refused his calls and returned his letters unopened. Pleas from family and friends to reconcile were met by me with a resounding *No* — a decision I felt was right.

The initial rupture in our relationship can be traced back to the period following my parents' divorce. I was ten, and he was thirty-five. Soon after, Edmund married the woman who would become my stepmother; I moved with them from a leafy neighborhood in the city to a small farm. Uprooted from my life, I was thrust into a tumultuous new world. At school, I thrived as an honor student, varsity athlete, and president of the student body, yet at home, I felt like a failure, unable to fit into the new family structure marked by unrealistic expectations and relentless criticism.

By fourteen, I started driving, and by fifteen, I saved enough to buy an old truck. But at sixteen, Edmund took it away, stripping me of my incipient, fragile independence. With nothing left to lose, I reached a turning point and decided to leave home in search of freedom and a future on my terms.

For six years, we did not exchange a word.

Then, in my twenties, a brush with cancer forced me to contact Edmund. The doctors gave me a one-in-three chance of survival, and I needed blood for a transfusion. This crisis brought us together, and we tried to rekindle our relationship. Still, despite our efforts, old wounds resurfaced, and we found ourselves at odds once more. I resigned myself to the belief that we might never speak again.

Ten more years passed. As I matured, I realized I could no longer ignore the conflict with Edmund. The tension had subtly and not so subtly influenced many aspects of my life. Allowing time to pass was no longer an option. I needed to take deliberate action. To break free, I had to strike out in a new direction, one not constrained by unanswered questions or lingering emotions. By applying the seven steps, I aimed to make peace with the past and chart a new course for the future.

Step 1: Ask The Question

The decision-making process begins with forming a clear question. The purpose of this step is twofold: to clarify the decision and illuminate potential answers. The most effective questions narrow the choice to two distinct options. Framing the issue as a binary, forced choice brings the stakes into sharp relief.

If the question does not evoke a sense of urgency or discomfort, it may signal the timing is not right or the question is not framed precisely enough. Take a moment to reconsider the question, as it may point to a broader challenge that needs addressing.

In my case, the question was straightforward: Should I (A) attempt to reestablish a relationship with my estranged father or (B) maintain the status quo, the absence of a relationship?

Step 2: Acknowledge Your Immediate Response

Having posed your question, take note of your immediate response, that first impulse or instinctive reaction. If possible, write it down but resist the urge to act on it immediately.

No matter how swift or seemingly irrational, your initial reaction warrants further examination. Acknowledge this response without rushing to judgment. It may reflect your immediate desires or could reveal unconscious patterns that subtly influence your behavior. For example, you might notice a tendency to avoid confrontation, react defensively, or freeze in moments of stress. You could also uncover habits such as people-pleasing, perfectionism, or seeking undue external validation.

Once the initial urge to react subsides, you can begin to explore other possibilities. Consider the strongest arguments for and against acting on your first impulse. Reflect on how this decision might affect those around you.

When I first considered reconnecting with Edmund, my immediate response was a resounding *No* or *Never*, with *Never* serving as a stand-in for *Not in the foreseeable future*. Years of distance and unresolved emotions made up a seemingly insurmountable barrier between us. The mere thought of reaching out filled me with dread and apprehension.

However, as I reflected further, I recognized that this initial trepidation stemmed from past pain and disappointment. Part of me longed for resolution, for a chance to understand and possibly forgive. Then, I began to consider the broader implications of reconnecting with Edmund. Would it bring peace and a sense of liberation, or would it only resurface painful memories? Moreover, how would this decision affect those closest to me, who had witnessed the toll the estrangement had taken over the years?

By thoughtfully examining the complex emotions and relationships involved, rather than simply following our first instinct, we position ourselves to make more informed and deliberate choices that align with our intentions and aspirations.

Step 3: Seek Perspective

This step broadens our understanding by considering the concerns, advice, and potential resistance from those affected by our decision. By acknowledging the limits of our individual viewpoint, we can uncover valuable insights and anticipate possible outcomes.

Make a list of individuals and groups most affected by your decision and consider the advice they might offer. For personal choices, this list might include immediate family or close friends. For work-related matters, consider including your supervisor, colleagues, clients, or business partners.

Still uncertain? Think about those whose lives intersect with yours and will directly, or indirectly bear the consequences or who should naturally be part of the conversation.

Next, imagine what advice each person or group might offer. Keep their possible responses brief — a sentence or two for each should suffice. Avoid overcomplicating your thinking.

In my case, I considered the potential advice of those most affected.

The list included close friends who had become like family over the years; my mother, who still harbored anger toward Edmund; Edmund's family, who wished to end the ongoing divide; and, to a lesser extent, colleagues and acquaintances who might have subtly sensed the unresolved tension in my life.

My close friends might suggest proceeding with caution and ensuring that I prioritize my emotional well-being while exploring the possibility of reconciliation. My mother, having experienced a turbulent relationship with Edmund, might advise against reopening old wounds and instead suggest focusing on the present and future. Our relatives might encourage reconciliation to bring peace to the family. Colleagues and acquaintances might be unaware of the history between Edmund and me. Still, they could likely sense the effect — the gap in my family history, the unending striving, the distrust of authority figures. They might advise finding a resolution as a step toward peace.

After imagining others' advice, consider what these individuals might not know. Reflect on any facts, motivations, or unspoken beliefs that, if shared, could change their perspectives. This step helps you identify potential blind spots in others' advice.

While many people derive their sense of identity from relationships, particularly family ties, I do not. I view relationships with parents, siblings, or children as largely independent; there is no familial pass for unacceptable behavior. There were also aspects of my relationship with Edmund that few understood, such as the circumstances behind our estrangement and the betrayal I felt. Most significantly, while Edmund may not have changed, I had, though, in all honesty, not entirely for the better. However, in recent years, I had made a deliberate effort to let go of the past, assert greater autonomy over my choices, and accept responsibility for them.

Finally, consider the objectivity and limitations of those most affected by your decision. It is easy to seek out people who merely affirm your views. Challenge yourself to identify those who might offer the most thought-provoking advice. Their experiences, biases, and desires can influence your perspective. For example, how might the advice of a protective parent differ from that of an adventurous friend?

I weighed the value of my emotional well-being against my desire for peace. What is the true cost of a troubled conscience? My unresolved relationship with Edmund had lingered for years, subtly altering my behavior. I found myself avoiding certain occasions, such as the funeral of his mother-in-law, whom I had regarded as a grandparent, and even his wife's. I began to wonder if we would ever see each other again or if our last goodbye had already been said.

Step 4: Envision Someone Wise

To broaden your perspective, consider the sources of wisdom around you. Identify individuals you respect for their insight and understanding: a trusted friend, a mentor, a family member with sound judgment, or a seasoned professional. This person could be someone you know, a historical figure, or even a fictional character. The ideal person brings wisdom gained through experience. Their advice is grounded in strong principles, open-mindedness, and empathy, always seeking the best for everyone involved.

For instance, a trusted friend or acquaintance who has successfully resolved a similar predicament could offer a unique perspective. Their story may differ from yours, but it could contain common themes or lessons, or provide unexpected insights.

Additionally, envision what your *future self* might advise. Picture yourself a decade or more into the future, enriched by the wisdom of experience. This *future you* understands your motivations better than anyone else ever could.

In my case, I turned to my friend Thomas, a consistent source of wisdom in my life. Like me, his background was modest, he had built a business, and he was now in a stage of reevaluating his life. Our friendship began in a structured leadership development class and grew through shared experiences in self-development courses and motorcycling across Europe. We had formed a strong bond over the previous two years. I placed more credibility in his insights, as we were both undergoing personal and professional transitions, and I had witnessed his thoughtful approach firsthand.

After identifying the wise figures in your life, consider the questions they might raise. They may ask what you truly want, what fears or doubts are holding you back, and which assumptions you have left unexamined. They may press you to consider how much this decision will matter over time, or what counsel you would offer a friend facing the same choice.

Your future self may frame the matter more plainly: What will this decision ask of you, and what will it cost if you do nothing? Will the direction you choose today allow you to live without regret?

When I brought my dilemma to Thomas, he first asked about the timeline of my estrangement from Edmund. He wanted to know when the relationship first became strained and whether I could identify the specific events that led to the rupture. He encouraged me to reflect on who I was then and who I am now, to better understand both Edmund's behavior and mine, and to recognize the combination of anger and fear that likely influenced us both.

Thomas then probed my reasoning for and against reconnecting with Edmund. He asked what I was willing to contribute to the relationship and what I hoped to gain from it. Would reconnecting require addressing unresolved issues? True to his nature, Thomas did not attempt to answer the question. Instead, he shared his experiences with family members who had come and gone in his life, the differences that divided them, the basis of his choices regarding whether to renew relationships, and how to reengage with them. As a true provocateur, Thomas prompted me to examine my selective memories, recognize narratives I had internalized, and articulate my aspirations. His approach exemplified the value of seeking perspective from others, as it challenged me to think more broadly about the decision.

Part of my *future self* envisioned letting go, questioning why I should bother speaking to Edmund again when memories of the past were painful and difficult to reconcile on my own. After all, I was content now. Why risk that? But a larger part of me also questioned the value of reconciliation or, at a minimum, closure. This hinted at the question behind the question: Was this about winning a struggle between a parent and child, or something more significant? Could a child grow up seeing all people, including his parents, as imperfect? More broadly, was this about extending grace?

Step 5: Engage the Voice of Wisdom

When faced with important decisions, the process often feels like a contest between the feelings of our body, the emotions of the heart, and the logic of the mind. However, the most reliable way to discern what is true and right is to pause and turn inward. Taking even a brief moment to pause interrupts habitual thought patterns and allows us to draw on the wisdom from all parts of our being — our whole intelligence, our intuition. Our voice of wisdom.

Let us do that now.

Set aside uninterrupted time and find a quiet space where you will not be disturbed. This could mean sitting alone, taking a walk in nature, or choosing a setting that allows you to relax and focus inward.

Begin by settling into a comfortable position. Let your back align naturally, and if it feels right, close your eyes. Take a slow, steady breath in, allowing the muscles of your body to relax as you exhale. Inhale deeply again, holding your breath for a few moments before releasing it in a gentle flow. Repeat this process once or twice, holding your breath for a count of five before letting it go. Then, let your breathing find its natural rhythm — in and out, in and out — flowing smoothly without effort.

Bring your attention to the sensation of each breath. You might focus on the rise and fall of your abdomen, the gentle lift of your chest, or the movement of air at your nostrils. Choose one point of focus and observe the inhalation and exhalation with quiet attention.

Continue to follow your breath, letting your mind settle and your body ease into stillness. As you breathe, you may notice a sense of calm spreading through you — beginning at the crown of your head, softening your forehead, relaxing your jaw, and easing your shoulders. Feel this wave of release move through your chest, abdomen, legs, and feet until your entire body feels at rest.

If (and when) distractions arise or your mind begins to wander, do not worry. Acknowledge these thoughts without judgment, letting them drift away as you gently redirect your focus back to your breath.

As you continue breathing, begin to notice the spaces between breaths, the moments when you are neither inhaling nor exhaling, like the intervals of silence in a piece of music. Observe the tranquility within fleeting instances of stillness. Allow this sense of serenity to flow through you during each pause.

Now, turn your attention inward to the center of your being. Rest your focus on the pauses between breaths, letting them gradually become longer and more peaceful. With each breath, feel yourself settling closer to the center of your body, your inner sanctuary, where you feel calm, centered, and relaxed. This is your place of tranquility.

Breathe in, pause, breathe out. Breathe in, pause, breathe out.

Within this quiet, still place, reconnect with the part of you that *knows*, the part that holds your history and has gained insight from your experiences. This is the part that understands your fears, hopes, intentions, and aspirations. It is the source of wisdom flowing through you, and it seeks to ensure your well-being and that of those around you.

Gently but firmly, hold your attention in this space and summon your full attention here. Be patient, trusting that the answer you seek is already present.

Remain here, open and attentive, *listening* for whatever arises. Although the voice of wisdom may not present itself as words or sounds, the answer will emerge. Which direction beckons you forward? Which choice seems uninviting? What new possibilities have revealed themselves?

Among the many voices in your mind, the voice of wisdom may be difficult to discern. It competes with the inner critic who doubts your decisions, an optimist who glosses over challenges, or a worrier who conjures scenes of failure. Echoes of authority figures — parents, teachers, or mentors — may replay their expectations or criticisms. Even the well-meaning suggestions of friends and family can add to the din. Amid this internal chorus, the tug of daily life asserts itself — work, family, and responsibilities — vie persistently for attention. To quiet these distractions, picture them as leaves floating down a stream or clouds drifting across the sky, gradually receding away as you return to the simplicity of your breath.

You will recognize the voice of wisdom when your body, heart, and mind align, affirming its truth. It will offer the thoughts, words, or actions suited to the circumstances. While the answer may not be immediately apparent, trust that you have initiated the process.

If the answer eludes you, try again later.

The voice of wisdom will persist, contemplating the question even when your conscious mind is not actively engaged with it. After an hour, a day, or even longer, the right answer will come to you suddenly. You will know its truth; the right course of action becomes crystal clear. The insight may arrive like a bolt of lightning, prompting an illuminating "Aha!" moment. Alternatively, it may gradually build over time like distant thunder — *Aaaah!* — accompanied by an unspoken inclination that gently propels you toward the nourishing light of the life you seek.

What did the voice of wisdom tell me?

In my case, the voice of wisdom whispered: "It is time to grow up." While my initial inclination had been *No* and *Never*, those responses stemmed from fear and self-protection. The voice of wisdom revealed that a meaningful step toward healing and reconciliation was necessary for my well-being. This insight illuminated the toll of our unresolved relationship — the lingering unease, unanswered questions, and the burden of the past. My heart yearned for resolution while my mind acknowledged the risks and obstacles ahead.

The first challenge was acknowledging the role of anger in my life. For so long, anger had been an inexhaustible source of energy, fueling my drive to prove my worth and succeed. It worked — I excelled in school and my career. But at what cost? Inevitably, anything born of negativity or delusion takes a toll on the person harboring those feelings. Behind this challenge, a larger question emerged: What if I could make peace with the past and truly let go? What would motivate me then? That question was more frightening to confront. Despite this, I felt a flicker of hope — a stronger desire to break free from the cycle of resentment, find closure, and ultimately achieve peace.

Listening to that inner guidance, I set out on a pursuit of self-discovery and transformation. Stripping away all the stories, I asked myself: Who am I? What do I value? What future do I want to create? This introspection led to a more comprehensive understanding of Edmund, myself, and our shared history, creating the conditions for a more fulfilling future.

Step 6: Act

Now that you know what you must do, how will you follow through?

The decision you have reached might require challenging yourself in unprecedented ways. Following through may involve taking a stand, initiating a difficult conversation, letting go, or offering an apology. It may also lead to meaningful changes in your life. Yet, if you have been honest with yourself in reaching this decision, sought perspective, and consulted the voice of wisdom, you will recognize that these challenges and discomforts are worth confronting.

To improve your chances of success, start by visualizing the result. What actions will you need to take? What outcome would you like to create?

In my case, as I contemplated contacting Edmund, the pull toward resolution was undeniable — not only regarding our relationship but also within myself. I wanted to address a matter that had long been unresolved. For a different outcome to occur, I would need to act.

The first step was to create a plan of action. I began by asking myself questions: What was at stake? How would I approach him? What would I say? How might he respond? And, most important, how could I relate to him differently now, viewing him through the lens of an adult, someone who no longer depended on him or had something to prove, rather than through the eyes of a child? I wanted to believe that with time, I had gained more compassion, for Edmund and others. These introspective queries helped me prepare for what might arise and how best to respond.

Next, I translated these reflections into a bulleted list of actionable tasks:

- Meet in person, as I wanted to be face-to-face.

- Choose a neutral location.

- Outline what I wanted to say.

Next, I considered what might complicate the exchange. Even a thoughtful plan can be tested in the moment. By imagining different turns the conversation might take, I prepared myself to respond rather than react.

With Edmund, I considered the difficult admissions I had made in the past about my shortcomings that may have contributed to the rupture in our relationship. I prepared myself for his potential responses — whether angry, contrite, or indifferent.

I then visualized the conversation, recognizing that emotional preparation was just as important as logistical planning. The best part of me needed to acknowledge the best in Edmund — this was fundamental to finding a resolution. I pictured myself speaking calmly and confidently, expressing my thoughts and feelings without accusation or defensiveness. I used self-affirming statements, reminding myself that I, too, was an adult, an equal, now in control of my life. There was nothing he could take from me, and I had the strength to listen and respond with maturity. These techniques helped build the emotional resilience I would need to address any potential challenges or difficult emotions that might arise during our conversation. Importantly, I reminded myself to listen openly to whatever he might say and to reserve judgment on what might follow.

After weeks — perhaps even years — of mental and emotional preparation, the moment had finally arrived. I called Edmund, bracing myself for any outcome. To my surprise, he agreed to meet.

We chose a restaurant midway between us, a neutral space for what might be a charged encounter. As I entered the parking lot, a strange realization struck me: I had no idea what car he might drive or how his appearance might have changed. Time had frozen him in my memory. When we finally spotted each other, we exchanged startled glances, both taken aback by how much was different while so much remained remarkably the same. Handshakes, strained greetings, and a walk into the restaurant were filled with questions about whether we had dined there before. The scent of garlic and baking bread hung in the air, a familiar yet unremarkable backdrop to our awkward reunion.

Once seated, the server wove through the room with practiced ease, her lively patter filling the space between hurried footsteps and the clatter of silverware. The small but necessary decisions around what to order offered a temporary distraction from the awkward solemnity of our meeting. But with our orders placed, a disquieting silence stretched between us. I found myself observing this man who had cast such a long shadow over my life, a figure once idealized, then resented, now simply human. There was no surge of nervousness but rather a detached recognition of two people sharing the same space. I had come with a quiet desire for resolution, holding an unspoken hope that something like peace might finally find its way between us. I felt startlingly calm, as if there was nothing to gain or lose, just two people attempting to reconcile a complex history. How to begin?

"I decided to grow up," I began, the words feeling heavy, a truth long overdue. "I held onto anger for so many years, but now . . . now I see you in another way: as a person, someone who also played a key role in my life." Continuing, I acknowledged the gifts he had unknowingly bestowed upon me: a sharp mind, a strong will, and a relentless drive. I also spoke to the reasons for my long silence — the need to make my way in the world, free from the past. With measured conviction, I shared a salient insight that transformed my worldview: the belief that, with rare exceptions, people are genuinely doing their best. We all want to make the right choices, even as we are each weighed down by the burdens of the past — successes and failures, heartbreaks, and unanswered questions. I suggested that perhaps I might understand him better now, recognizing that he, too, was simply approaching life and making the best choices he could at the time, even as he struggled with questions about his father's love.

Edmund listened attentively as I spoke. He seemed to be taking it in, sometimes affirming and sometimes demurring. When he spoke, he was self-critical and quick to credit others for their role in my upbringing. Finally, he admitted his wish that he had been a better father, his words laced with unvarnished regret. Most touchingly, he offered the kind acknowledgment a child hopes to receive for their accomplishments.

As he spoke, a sudden realization took hold: Parents, too, seek their children's approval. However, the role of being a parent is far more complex than that of being a child. Parents make decisions that govern their children's lives while seeking future validation and acceptance from the very beings they are responsible for nurturing. This insight shed new light on my relationship with Edmund and the challenges he faced as a father.

By the evening's end, I made my intentions clear: a fresh start, a friendship tentatively offered. His response, a flicker of warmth in his eyes, hinted at the possibility of hope.

As we walked toward the parking lot, he abruptly halted. In a gesture neither of us could have predicted, we embraced for the first time in our adult lives. It was a hug born not of dramatic reconciliation but rather of sober acknowledgment between two people who share a common bond of living through trying times together. With an unspoken understanding of leaving the past behind, we promised to meet again and continue exploring what the future might hold for us as friends.

This experience reminded me that, in situations like this, expecting yourself to devise a solution for every potential challenge may be unrealistic. However, by formulating expectations about those hurdles and how you might address them, you give yourself the ability to adapt when necessary. The objective is to remain flexible and resilient in the face of these challenges.

As you begin to act, remember that setbacks and obstacles are a natural part of the process. By staying true to your inner wisdom, preparing thoroughly, and accepting the discomfort of the unknown, you open yourself to new possibilities. Trust in your ability to confront any challenges, knowing that each obstacle you overcome brings you closer to your goals. With persistence and commitment, you can achieve success and fulfillment in all areas of your life.

Step 7: Observe and Adapt

The decision-making process continues beyond the initial action. Ensuring your choices lead to the intended outcomes requires maintaining ongoing awareness, monitoring your behavior, and reflecting on results to adjust how you proceed.

Pay attention to your actions. Assess whether they align with your intentions and adjust based on what you learn. Observing in real-time might seem daunting, but it is likely a skill you already use instinctively. Consider how often you choose your words, what to say or not say, and monitor your tone of voice. To make this more intentional, focus your attention, not to become overly self-conscious but to notice and learn.

Reflection, too, is a natural practice. Consider how often you think about a recent conversation or event. Bring structure to this process. For example, set aside a few minutes at the end of each day or week to capture the lessons you have learned. You can also integrate this practice into activities that allow your mind to wander, such as exercising or commuting.

As you reflect, consider both the decision and the process. For future choices, ask yourself: Did I rush through any part of the process? Did I overanalyze to the point of inaction? Use these insights to pinpoint areas for adjustment and sharpen your abilities over time.

My decision to contact Edmund yielded valuable insights. While many lessons related to my personal history, two stand out for their applicability. The first lesson, which I believe to be universally true, is: *In some way, each of us feels disadvantaged by the past.* Whether through circumstances beyond our control or personal struggles carried over from childhood, we all carry the invisible imprints of what came before. If you look back at almost anyone's history, you can trace the line they have traveled from the limitations of their beginnings to the unheralded ways they have risen beyond them in maturing into adults. Some of us attempt to ignore these burdens, while others drown them in distractions or overcompensate in their quest to break free. And some, perhaps the bravest among us, confront them directly.

Consider Edmund, for example. Born in the shadow of war, he suffered from debilitating asthma that deprived him of the carefree joys of childhood. His father, having served his country, returned home a changed man, one who struggled to truly understand or nurture his young son. As Edmund grew older, he was eventually sent away to military school and left to face adulthood on his own. Though he tried to outrun it, the past always lingered, a shadow from which he could never fully escape.

This brings us to the second, closely related lesson: *Our minds are never fully unburdened until we make peace with that past.* No matter how far we travel or how high we rise, the unresolved remains tethered to us, influencing every decision and reaction. It is only when we confront and reconcile the wounds of our history that we can begin to experience true freedom. Peace does not come simply with the passage of time but through the deliberate act of understanding and acceptance.

By integrating these lessons, we can overcome obstacles, seize opportunities, and rise to new heights with each successive decision and experience. This process is essential not only for our survival but also for our progress and success.

As for my relationship with Edmund, I no longer worry about whether we will communicate again. My focus has turned to strengthening the connection we now have, loosening the grip of the past, and choosing to see the best in him. This is about building a relationship that feels right for both of us. Meeting him as he is, rather than as I imagined him to be, marked the true change. While writing this book, I invited him on a weeklong trip to a destination of his choice. He chose Paris.

Summary

Chapter 10, "A Time to Practice," turns from explanation to application, inviting use of the seven steps through a decision that has been lingering or left unresolved. Insight alone is not enough. What matters is bringing the process into contact with lived experience, allowing choices to be tested through action and reconsidered through reflection. When decisions are carried into the world, patterns that were invisible in thought begin to show themselves. With repetition, the process becomes more familiar and reliable, strengthening confidence in one's ability to meet uncertainty, follow through, and act with intention rather than hesitation. As you reflect on this chapter, consider the following questions:

1. When and where could you set aside uninterrupted time to work through an important decision?
2. What decision have you been carrying but not addressing?
3. If you applied the seven steps to that decision, where would you begin today?
4. Which step tends to come easily for you, and which step do you tend to avoid or rush??
5. If you practiced this process regularly, how might your approach to difficult choices change over time?

Challenges

Self-Discovery: Set aside fifteen minutes to consider a decision that has been weighing on you. Work through steps 1 through 5, writing one to three sentences for each step. After completing the fifth step, read your responses from beginning to end. How did placing the decision within a clear structure affect your thinking, and how did this process clarify your understanding or bring you closer to an answer?

Further Exploration: Identify a friend, family member, or colleague who is facing a difficult choice. Without referencing the seven-step process, guide the conversation with open-ended questions: what options they are considering, which option they feel most drawn toward, and who may be affected by the decision. As you listen, resist the urge to solve the problem. Continue asking clarifying questions that help them articulate their thinking. Afterward, reflect on what you noticed about your role when you set aside advising and focused solely on listening.

Chapter 11 — Living Wisely

And this idea of good, like the sun, is also the cause of
growth, and the author not of knowledge only, but of being,
yet greater far than either in dignity and power.
—Plato[38]

Congratulations on arriving at this pivotal juncture. You have achieved more than a mere milestone — you have adopted a new decision-making approach and already begun to apply it. While it may be tempting to stop here, content with an intellectual grasp of the process — many do[39] — wisdom calls for more. Wisdom is not a peak to scale and leave behind; it requires ongoing reciprocity and active engagement. To do this, you must live wisely.

But what does it mean to live wisely? The answer lies in our commitment to pursue wisdom with intention, practice it in our choices, and share it with others.

The pursuit of wisdom is a relentless quest for truth that expands your understanding and challenges the limits of what you know. It requires curiosity, reflection, and humility. Wisdom reveals the complexity of life, showing that the more you learn, the more you see the boundaries of your knowledge. By reading this book and engaging with its seven steps, you have already started on this process. Yet this is just the beginning.

Practicing wisdom means making conscious, ethical choices in every situation, no matter how difficult. We integrate thoughtful decision-making into our lives. Each time you apply these seven steps, or any mindful process, to the dilemmas you encounter, you practice wisdom.

Participating in wisdom goes beyond individual practice. It involves exchanging ideas that enrich our lives and the lives of those

around us. By sharing insights, we help one another approach decisions with greater care and conviction. By offering reflections and
encouraging thoughtful choices, we contribute to a shared understanding that strengthens over time.

In these interactions, we become increasingly attuned to the
wisdom in others. We see Aaron as a beacon of well-being, Henri
as a paragon of family commitment, Cathryn as the embodiment of
nurturing love, Jon as a fount of insightful questions, and Sofia as a
master of attentive listening. Together, they remind us that wisdom
is not abstract but lived, carried from person to person through ordinary presence and example.

Now, let us examine each stage of this transformation and
consider how pursuit, practice, and participation work together.

Pursue

To pursue wisdom is to step beyond familiar patterns, question
received assumptions, and expand our understanding of what is
true. It begins not with certainty but with a decision to let wisdom
guide us. Wisdom does not reside solely in books or traditions; it
arises in the texture of ordinary life. It reveals itself in daily decisions, conversations, and moments of simply being. What initiates
the pursuit is not intellect alone but a posture of openness, a willingness to seek broader perspectives and to understand them with
care. By resisting the pull of familiar thought, we engage more fully
with our surroundings. We challenge what we think we know. We
explore what we do not. In doing so, we open ourselves to a fuller
grasp of life and our place within it.

While wisdom is not confined to the province of traditional learning alone, some sources offer timeless treasures. Reading widely
— whether philosophy, history, literature, or science — provides a
foundation for thoughtful inquiry. Books extend our vision, offering
windows into the minds of great thinkers. They broaden judgment,

stir reflection, and ask us to revisit our assumptions about truth and meaning.

Structured learning also plays a vital role. Courses, seminars, and lectures create opportunities to confront complexity, test ideas, and develop discernment. Studying history, engaging with ethical theories, or tracing intellectual traditions does more than expand knowledge — it compels us to grapple with unfamiliar questions and challenge our assumptions. In doing so, we strengthen our capacity to reason carefully, communicate clearly, and understand more fully. Traditional education, at its best, trains us not only to learn but to ask what learning is for.

Yet wisdom does not confine itself to academic settings; it is woven into the fabric of ordinary surroundings. Nature, with its measured pace and subtle rhythms, offers lasting insight for those who attend closely. Consider a tree — its roots anchored in soil, its branches reaching skyward — offering a lesson in balance. The arc of a river, bending and carving through stone, shows how persistence reshapes what once seemed fixed. Or the migration of birds, directed by instinct rather than instruction, reveals that true guidance need not be visible to be real. These images instruct not through explanation but through presence. Nature, when regarded with care, becomes a patient teacher — grounded, enduring, and true.

Just as nature imparts lessons, so do those around us. Every individual carries a story, a perspective, an insight waiting to be offered. A friend's reflection, the casual remark from a barista, or a grandparent's recollection — any of these might reframe a question you believed settled. These brief encounters can alter our thinking and expand our view. The insight may arrive without fanfare, even without words, yet it lingers. The task is not to search for wisdom but to stay receptive. More often than not, the most enduring truths come from unremarkable voices, heard not because they speak loudly but because we are listening.

Conversation, in particular, provides fertile ground for understanding. These exchanges need not take place in formal settings. The most revealing often do not. A question over dinner, a shared walk, a passing remark on a commute — any of these can unsettle a settled thought. Enter each conversation not to convince but to understand. No one sees the whole. Each of us holds a fragment of the larger picture. When we gather those fragments with care, a fuller view begins to emerge, not because it is unified but because it is layered.

What conversation offers in dialogue, travel offers in encounter. Immersing ourselves in unfamiliar surroundings shifts our perspective in ways that words alone cannot. Imagine stepping into a foreign city for the first time: the air thick with unfamiliar scents, the streets winding like a labyrinth, the sounds of a language you do not speak buzzing around you. Local delicacies tempt your palate, offering a taste of the region's culinary traditions. Immersed in the unknown, we see the world through a new lens. These moments, whether in bustling city streets or the quiet corners of a remote village, invite us to reconsider our assumptions, offering a richer understanding of the human experience.

Culture, too, teaches. Traditions, languages, and rituals carry memory and meaning, reservoirs of insight refined across generations. By immersing ourselves in these practices, whether familiar or new, we glimpse the frameworks by which others understand their lives. This kind of learning does not require expertise. It asks only for attention and regard. In return, it reveals lessons in resilience, community, and the variety of human expression. These encounters remind us not only of difference but of kinship and the many ways people across time and place have searched for meaning and made sense of their world.

To pursue wisdom is not merely to gather facts. It is the willingness to be altered, perhaps even transformed, by what we encounter. The transformation is internal. It requires ongoing effort to meet the world with reflection and receptivity. We must approach each one with the willingness to be changed. This kind of engagement calls on us to set aside assumptions, to listen, and to ask not only what we saw but what it taught us. When what we learn alters what we see, and what we see begins to guide our choices, understanding becomes not only possible but real.

With time, we begin to see that truth is not fixed but filtered, by perspective and season. While some principles remain, our understanding of them evolves. A truth seen from one vantage may appear differently from another. What felt certain in one season may reveal new layers when reconsidered in another. A book, a conversation, or a new environment can cause us to question what we thought we knew, not by contradicting it but by recasting its meaning. When we remain open in this way, we are able to hold multiple perspectives and honor the complexity of human experience.

Even so, some principles endure. While history or context may lead to differing conclusions, we can agree on the qualities required for sound judgment: attentiveness, humility, and a willingness to question what we think we know. When we return to these commitments again and again, they become habits. In that repetition, seeking understanding gives way to practice.

Practice

Be honest with yourself. How often have books, conversations, or moments of insight stirred resolve, only for it to fade? The spark of recognition can feel powerful in the moment, even convincing. It conveys the energy of possibility. Yet recognition alone does not change behavior. Without follow-through, it remains an idea rather than action, like locating a treasure on a map and never setting out to claim it. Real transformation arises from the consistent application of what we learn, repeated often enough to alter how we behave.

This is true for artists and professionals as it is for becoming a wise decision-maker. Only through disciplined repetition do the fundamentals become second nature. It is how skill strengthens and judgment becomes more reliable.

Consider this process akin to learning an instrument. Miles Davis did not become a jazz virtuoso simply by picking up a trumpet and improvising at will. He devoted countless hours working through foundational exercises, learning structure, and training his hands to follow what his mind could hear long before he began to improvise. The same holds true across disciplines. What appears effortless from the outside is almost always the result of long familiarity earned through sustained practice. Decision-making is no exception. It improves not through a single realization but through continued use. Only by applying what we know, again and again, do the fundamentals become available when we need them most.

Proficiency itself rarely progresses along a straight line. Periods of momentum are often followed by plateaus or apparent regression. This is not a sign that the work has failed but evidence that learning is underway. Success highlights what fits the situation well. Failure exposes assumptions that deserve reexamination. Both are instructive. What feels like stagnation is often a period of integration, when experience is absorbed before it can be expressed in a new way.

Consistency is vital. Just as a musician develops fluency through daily practice, sound judgment develops by engaging the process again and again. This applies not only to major decisions but to ordinary ones: how you manage your time, how you respond in conversation, how you follow through on small commitments. These moments accumulate. In each case, repetition gives way to automatic response. Thought and action become coordinated. What once required conscious effort becomes available because the process has been rehearsed.

Decision-making follows the same arc. Through practice, the process no longer feels external or imposed. It becomes accessible, even automatic. Choices that once required deliberate effort begin to form with greater ease, even as the stakes remain the same. What changes is not the importance of the decision, but your relationship to the process of making it. Attention shifts from managing the steps to engaging the moment.

The seven steps themselves are not rules to be followed mechanically but a guide. They exist to support decision-making, not to replace it. Some decisions may call for every step; others only a few. The point is discernment: knowing which steps matter most in the moment. A choice may require no more than brief attention, or it may call for deliberate pacing and broader perspective. These variations are not departures from the process; they are signs that it is being applied with judgment.

Grasping the seven steps is only a starting point. Real proficiency develops as you make the process your own. Mastery in any field requires learning the fundamentals, yes, and something more. It moves beyond faithful imitation through intuition, experimentation, and the gradual emergence of your own style. The same holds true with wisdom. The steps provide an initial structure, a way in, not a final form. You may rely on certain steps more than others, reorder them, or introduce elements of your own. What matters is not adherence to a method, but forming a way of deciding that fits how you think, choose, and live.

This is the promise of sustained practice. Over time, deliberate effort arrives naturally, guided by intention rather than impulse. You become more alert and more prepared, even when conditions are unclear. Attention shifts from simply reaching an outcome to understanding how that outcome was reached.

But perhaps most important, practice opens the way for something larger. It prepares you to offer your insight to others. What begins as a personal effort becomes a shared responsibility, not to instruct or prescribe, but to contribute. Wisdom is not only for the self. It is meant to be lived and, in time, passed on.

Participate

Life is brimming with challenges universal to the human experience: pondering existence, seeking purpose, confronting loss, and making moral decisions. These struggles connect us across time and culture. Consider the *Tao Te Ching*, a text written thousands of years ago. Open its pages now, and it may seem as though it was written to address questions of our current age. This enduring power of wisdom affirms not only our shared human condition but the value of what has been passed down to help us meet it.

While life's enduring challenges persist, the world continues to evolve at a remarkable pace. New technologies alter how we work, how we relate, and how we understand ourselves. The complexities of modern life exceed what any one person can manage alone. Either billions of us attempt to solve them in isolation, or better, we help each other. This is not an act of charity; it is a contribution to the common good. In exchanging what we have learned, we build on what others began and strengthen it for those to follow.

After practicing wisdom in our own lives, the next step is to share it. Participation involves more than passing along ideas. It means living what we have learned, recognizing the potential for insight in others, and creating conditions where mutual understanding can grow. Wisdom does not exist apart from us; it advances through our actions and is carried forward in the way we speak, the choices we make, and the encouragement we offer. Each time we do this, through conversation, example, or grounded support, we help make the world more compassionate, more thoughtful, and more wise.

Wisdom does not end with what has been handed down. It continues to evolve through us. As we live, reflect, and respond to our time, our experiences become part of its ongoing expression. By adding our voice, not only by what we say but by how we live, we extend what came before and prepare it for what lies ahead.

Yet we cannot share what we do not understand. And we cannot act wisely on behalf of others without first clarifying what we hold true. That begins with a personal moral code, a framework for choosing in alignment with our principles. It offers steadiness when desire, doubt, or pressure pull in different directions. It draws belief and behavior into coherence, helping us act with consistency — not only when the choice is clear but especially when it is not.

A moral code sharpens self-understanding and builds trust in our relationships. It allows us to meet difficult moments without hesitation, knowing our decisions reflect more than preference or convenience. They reflect what we hold to be true. This is the grounding from which we speak with confidence, not only that our choices are good but that they are right. Not only for us but for those whose lives our choices touch.

There is an important distinction here between ethics and morality. Ethics are often prescribed, defined by institutions, laws, or religious doctrines. For example, the Ten Commandments guided actions in many religious communities; today, legal codes shape societal conduct. A moral code, by contrast, is personal. It draws on external sources but is assembled through internal reflection. It evolves over time, clarified in practice, tested by experience, and guided by judgment. How we apply its principles, not just what we inherit but what we prove through living, is what makes it ours.

The sources of a moral code vary. A Christian might look to the teachings of the Bible, as often read in the King James Version. A Taoist might live by the principle of *wu wei*, or effortless action. A humanist might draw on Bertrand Russell's *A Liberal Decalogue*. Most people take an eclectic approach, blending influences from religious texts, philosophical ideas, literature, cultural traditions, and personal experience. Your code might include love of neighbor, reverence for nature, stewardship of resources, honesty in action, or dignity toward all people. What matters is not where it comes from but whether it helps you choose well. The sources vary, but the aim is the same: to live with integrity when it matters most.

Even the clearest principles demand attention in their application. Honesty, for instance, is widely upheld as a virtue, from the Ten Commandments to the US Military Academy's Cadet Honor Code, but its meaning varies with context. Would you tell the truth if it would cause unnecessary harm? Would you lie about someone's whereabouts to protect them from danger? These are not abstract hypotheticals. They reveal what it means to act with moral conscience: to weigh values, intentions, and consequences when no clear solution exists.

Through articulating your moral code, you enrich your understanding of virtue and contribute to a larger discourse on ethical living. This dialogue expands our collective understanding of what it means to live a life of integrity. It does not require credentials or consensus, only a willingness to take responsibility for your choices and remain open to the insight others can offer. In doing so, wisdom becomes something shared.

You might contribute by documenting thoughtful responses to complex questions, synthesizing ideas across disciplines, or offering frameworks for ethical reasoning. You might study how people make decisions or facilitate exchanges that draw from multiple traditions and lived experiences. However, the most meaningful way to expand our shared wisdom is by helping others directly: by asking a thoughtful question, telling a meaningful story, or pausing long enough to listen.

Our instinct to help others is part of what makes us human. From the beginning, we have survived not only by solving problems but by passing along what we learned. We care for one another, we offer guidance, we tell stories. Each time we share what experience has taught us, we light the way for someone else. The result is not a perfect world but a more thoughtful one, bound by understanding and held together by care.

As we grow in understanding, we begin to look beyond our progress. We hope others might avoid mistakes we have made and go further than we have gone. Sharing the wisdom we have gathered is a form of generosity, not a matter of convincing or correcting but of offering. It means listening with care, asking thoughtful questions, and honoring the insight others carry within them.

Imagine yourself as a lamppost at the edge of a street. Your light does not prescribe a direction; it illuminates the surroundings, offering warmth and reassurance to those making their way forward. Serving others is not about offering conclusions. It is about creating an atmosphere where questions can be asked, and heard. When we listen without rushing to respond, we create space for others to think more clearly and choose more wisely.

Now picture a moment in the middle of a demanding day. You are focused on your own responsibilities, when someone nearby asks for your perspective. You could respond quickly and return to your task. Or you could pause. Ask a question. Listen fully. In the act of helping them sort through their thoughts, you may find your own becoming clearer as well. What begins as support for another becomes a kind of reckoning, a way of seeing your own decisions anew.

Helping others in this way is not a detour from practice. It is its continuation. The wisdom you offer is not something separate from your growth. The questions you raise and the care you extend do not deplete your reserves. They renew them.

Wisdom fulfills its purpose only when it is shared. Not by instruction but by presence. What you offer, in curiosity, compassion, and creativity, becomes part of what others carry forward. It is how we extend light into the lives of others. Not as a spotlight but as a steady invitation to see more clearly.

Summary

Chapter 11, "Living Wisely," presents wisdom not as something possessed once and for all but as something sustained through active engagement. Wisdom remains alive only when it is exercised. It begins with pursuit, a commitment to learning through attention to what is observed and lived. It continues through practice, applying judgment to real decisions and attending to what follows. It extends through participation, offering what you have learned and recognizing wisdom already present in others. Through this shared effort, you become wiser over time, and the body of wisdom itself grows. As you reflect on this chapter, consider the following questions:

1. Where do you notice wisdom in your daily life?

2. How, if at all, do you currently pursue wisdom?

3. What principles guide your decisions when no clear answer presents itself?

4. How might you adapt the seven-step process to better support the decisions you encounter?

5. In what ways can you offer what you have learned to others without directing them?

Challenges

Self-Discovery: Reflect on the past day. Identify three instances in which you noticed wisdom, whether in nature, in interactions with others, or in brief moments of awareness. For each, note what you observed and what it suggested about judgment, restraint, care, or attention. Then consider how this awareness informs your pursuit of wisdom and how it guides how you live wisely.

Further Exploration: Talk with someone you respect about how they try to improve their decision-making over time. Ask what practices help them learn from experience and adjust their behavior. Reflect on which of these practices you could apply more consistently in your life.

Chapter 12 — Becoming a Bearer of Light

One does not become enlightened by imagining figures of light, but by making the darkness conscious.
—Carl Jung[40]

As our exploration draws to a close, I feel compelled to make a disclosure. At the outset, I shared that the practices described in this book rest on three foundational premises: We are capable of making choices; our bodies, hearts, and minds are each sources of wisdom; and making the right choices leads to a better life. Yet there is a fourth premise, one that has implicitly supported this entire work. It is this: Our purpose — yours, mine, and every human being's — is to express love. And we do so, each of us, in our unique way. While you need not accept this premise to understand or apply the ideas presented in this book, it has been the central motivation for its creation.

People often view purpose as something elusive, a hidden treasure waiting to be discovered. However, I submit that purpose is a choice we make. It is not a fixed ideal existing *out there* but rather a construct we create in our minds (and hearts) to give our lives meaning and direction. Given this perspective, what could be more meaningful than expressing love? Put simply: to love.

Still, we often forget this fundamental truth. Or perhaps no one ever taught us.

From the moment we begin to learn language, we start to become molded into rational beings. Education rewards us for logic and reasoning. Later, work reinforces this emphasis on rationality. We become increasingly distanced from the spontaneity of the natural world, the richness of human connection, and the value of creativity.

A machine can produce an almost infinite number of mechanically perfect replicas of a painting by Picasso for only a few dollars each. And the original, with its smudges and misshapen figures lacking even a single straight line? Priceless.

Nonetheless, we have strayed from our essential nature in the quest for order, pattern, and design. Yet there is a way back: through wisdom. For the sum of all wisdom is love.

Love itself is a power beyond the grasp of the conscious mind. It is a unifying force without an opposite. It is not merely about tenderness and compassion; it equally embodies strength and perseverance. Love provides the will to transcend in the presence of resistance. If we possess any extraordinary power, it is love.

While this notion might initially seem surprising, consider your experiences. Reflect on the decisions you have made. If you were to ask yourself, "What were the most loving choices?" would this not guide you toward the better option? Inevitably, the right choice is the most loving choice.

A personal anecdote illustrates this point. For the better part of twelve years, I shared my life with Superdog. Our bond was unshakable, brought to life not only through moments of joy and play — walking together, running together, racing up stairs, wrestling on the floor, and hugging it up after — but also through my responsibility to care for her. As Superdog aged, she first contracted cancer, then a long-term, incurable respiratory disease, and finally began to lose her ability to walk. Caring for her required an increasing level of attention and adapting to her changing needs: administering a complex cocktail of medications, subjecting her to frequent (and expensive) testing, and providing periodic emergency intervention. For the last months of her life, I covered the floors of the house with yoga mats for her safety and fitted her with a diaper. I carried her up and down stairs and slept beside her, but her pain became increasingly obvious. Ultimately, the most difficult yet loving decision was to end her suffering. The vet eventually said it was time and came to the house to see Superdog through it. When she passed, I wept uncontrollably. To this day, I keep her collar on my desk as a reminder of our time together.

Wisdom, in all its dimensions, can inform our decisions. The best of these, however, are guided by love. And love, in all its expressions, is inseparable from wisdom.

The Light in Everyone We Meet

At the outset, we asked why, of all the stars in the universe, you should choose wisdom to guide your life. The answer becomes clear: Just as light pierces the darkest night, wisdom dispels doubt and confusion, revealing truth and guiding us toward what is right. Wisdom safeguards our well-being and leads us to fulfillment. Like the Sun, its radiant counterpart in the natural world, wisdom sustains life, offering the warmth and vitality that nurture all living things on Earth.

Yet the light of wisdom resides within us. After all, we are made of stardust. By choosing to live wisely, we align with those dedicated to the highest form of moral formation, making a commitment that mirrors the essence of our intellectual and ethical evolution. As we embody this way of being, we undergo a profound transformation. No longer mere seekers of wisdom, we become bearers of light, part of a constellation that illuminates the way for others.

Bearers of light are all around us. They are the patient teacher whose thoughtful guidance helped us, the attentive friend who listened, or the colleague whose passion for learning ignited our curiosity. Consciously or unconsciously, we are drawn to these individuals. They possess a luminous quality: a sparkle in their eyes, warmth in their presence, and an unwavering sense of calm, regardless of circumstance. Encountering them brings a sense of peace; their self-assurance and open-mindedness restore our optimism.

However, recognizing these bearers of light requires seeing beyond the surface. It means perceiving the beauty, truth, and goodness within each person we encounter and acknowledging the sacred fire that burns within them. As we recognize this light in others, we are reminded of our potential to be a source of light. Just as we are drawn to their wisdom, we, too, can inspire and guide those around us, becoming the very presence we seek. Honoring this light in others ignites the sacred fire within.

Revealing Your Inner Light

Each of us holds the potential to be a bearer of light. By engaging with this book, you have already begun the work of pursuing wisdom and uncovering the light within you.

This work is not about achieving perfection; none of us is flawless. Even the wisest among us are subject to sudden anger, carry unexamined biases, or feel a persistent longing for circumstances to be different. Nor does life always offer straightforward choices. We contend with uncertainty, confront decisions that test our resolve, and face moments when the way forward is obscured. Yet we strive, stumble, and, if we remain open, we learn.

Still, life, in its imperfections, offers an extraordinary gift: it is a place of practice, a proving ground for becoming a wiser, more intentional decision-maker. As your wisdom expands, the rewards are boundless.

You begin to recognize what truly matters, gaining insight into what is significant and letting trivial concerns fall away. You become more comfortable with ambiguity, accepting that life rarely offers clear answers. The need to compare fades; you no longer measure one situation against another or one person against another. You free yourself from the grip of societal expectations and others' judgments, living a life that feels unmistakably yours.

With time, wisdom steadies your inner compass. You begin to rely on the insights gained through experience, meeting challenges with grace and seeing each obstacle as an opportunity to strengthen resilience and understanding.

While these changes are meaningful, the most far-reaching consequence of living wisely is discovering the question behind all questions: What truly drives my choices? For me, the question is this: Are my decisions guided by fear or by love?

This question holds personal significance for me because, for much of my life, fear was a dominant force festering quietly beneath the surface. Outwardly, my choices may have seemed confident, even bold, yet beneath that carefully constructed image, fear subtly influenced many of my decisions. When it did surface, as it inevitably would, it manifested as anger. More often, though, it took a less overt form: a relentless need for control. That control provided the illusion of stability while paradoxically pulling me further from reality.

A good example of this played out in my professional life. As the manager of a law firm, I once placed a sign on the paper shredder that read *Suggestion Box*. Some colleagues laughed, but the message was unmistakable: Others' opinions were unwelcome. Why? Because to admit I needed input might reveal I did not have all the answers, or worse, that I needed to change.

In shutting out other perspectives, I began to build a narrative that suited my desires. I wanted to believe my decisions were correct, that my version of events was reality. Without feedback, there was no one to challenge this story. And so I clung to it, convinced it was true. But wanting something to be true does not make it so. How often do we tell ourselves stories that justify our actions, only to ignore the obvious signals that something is amiss? You can ignore the signs for a while, but eventually, the truth catches up.

For me, it came all at once. My career, my marriage, and the carefully constructed image of strength I had clung to all crumbled. The truths I had avoided, the perspectives I had dismissed, came rushing in like a tide, sweeping away the illusions I had built. Forced to confront the fear that had influenced so many of my decisions, I found myself in the wreckage, sifting through what remained of the life I thought I controlled.

What I discovered in that wreckage was the alternative to fear: love.

Love, unlike fear, does not demand control. It does not close itself off or cling to certainty. Love invites openness, vulnerability, and trust. Turning toward love has transformed my approach to life and work. I now seek out others' viewpoints, valuing them as much as or even more than mine. This is not merely an act of humility but an acknowledgment of the wisdom that resides within each of us.

It has also recast my life in subtler ways. I am less preoccupied with possessions and more drawn to the simplicity of the environment around me. I lose myself in the vastness of the sky, in the distant call of a bird, or in the way sunlight casts shifting patterns across a wall. In these moments, I feel tethered to something larger, sensing a light not only within myself but in everything, a light that has always been there, waiting patiently to be seen.

Maybe you see it too. Or perhaps you are still searching.

What Choice Will You Make?

Every great story involves a hero and a guide. The pursuit of wisdom mirrors this classic arc, a timeless narrative that echoes through our collective imagination. The hero answers the call to adventure, enters the unknown, overcomes trials, and returns transformed. However, the pursuit of wisdom is different. It does not end with a single triumphant return. For those who commit, the quest is unending. Each new challenge brings fresh insight, and with it, the chance to become more wholly oneself.

Moreover, unlike the hero's trumpet call, the invitation to live wisely is often subtle and nearly imperceptible. It may arrive as a flicker of awareness, a lingering question, or a sudden pause. It can surface when you face an irrevocable decision, reflect on past choices, or find yourself at the edge of a new beginning. However it comes, answering the call can feel daunting. Yet the process begins with a single, deliberate choice: to live wisely.

This choice transcends personal gain. It is not about getting ahead. It is about joining something far greater, a tradition that stretches across centuries and cultures. In taking it up, you begin the work of uncovering the light within that has illuminated the human story for millennia. You take on the abiding presence of the celestial bodies we once looked to as guides. You become part of what sustains and extends this inheritance, a universe still expanding, lit by every life that seeks to understand.

Of course, even with the noblest intention, you will fall short. We all do. These moments are not failures but invitations: to return, to learn, and to begin again. And each time you do, your light brightens.

There are no shortcuts, no guaranteed signs. While the road ahead may sometimes feel solitary, you are not alone. If you do feel that way, remember the fourth step in the process: having a conversation with someone wise. When you do, and if you remain open, you may be surprised by who appears. Wisdom often speaks through voices we did not anticipate, arriving at moments we least expect.

To ignore this call is not without consequence. Turning away from wisdom carries its own cost: missed opportunities, narrowing horizons, and a gradual erosion of meaning. The decision to pursue wisdom, or to delay it, is not abstract. In so choosing, you alter your experience of time, your relationships, your sense of purpose. So ask yourself plainly: Will you let your light shine?

Just as each star adds brilliance to the night sky, your pursuit of wisdom — whether a faint flicker or a steady flame — becomes a source of warmth and illumination for those around you.

So now, as you close this book, consider the questions before you:

Will you answer the call?

Will you take your place among those who have walked this noble path?

Only you can make this important decision for your life.

The next chapter of this story remains unwritten.

But the author has always been known.

Summary

Chapter 12, "Becoming a Bearer of Light," frames wisdom as an expression of love made visible through choice. Within each of us resides the capacity to become a bearer of light, someone who, through embodying wisdom, passes on the sacred fire to others. Fulfilling this potential requires a conscious commitment to choosing what is true and right, especially when doing so is difficult. As fear loosens its hold, decisions are increasingly guided by love. This choice may be the most consequential choice of a life, for it determines not only how you live but how your life enters the lives of others. As you reflect on this chapter, consider the following questions:

1. Who are some bearers of light who have influenced your life?

2. What specific qualities do you admire in these individuals?

3. Which of these same qualities do you already express in your choices or conduct?

4. How would living as a bearer of light change how you live today?

5. How might living as a bearer of light influence others' remembrance of you?

Challenges

Self-Discovery: Reflect on one decision you made in the past day, large or small. Consider what guided the choice in the moment and whether it was closer to fear or love, and notice how it affected you and those around you. What does this decision reveal about the light you express through your actions, and how might you choose with greater intention tomorrow.

Further Exploration: Identify someone you consider a bearer of light. Ask how they approach significant decisions, what principles guide them, and how they respond to uncertainty. Notice the qualities they demonstrate as they speak. Reflect on what you learn and consider how you might apply one of these practices in your life.

Lifelong Practice: Invite two or more people who share a commitment to living wisely to form a small circle for shared reflection and counsel. Meet regularly to discuss decisions you are facing and how you are meeting them. Encourage curiosity, compassion, and creativity in the exchange. Return often to the question of whether your actions are guided by love. Over time, observe how these conversations influence the quality of your decisions, and how they alter the way you live.

Epilogue

Two people play pivotal roles in the personal narrative that runs through this work, both of whom served as my teachers. One is my former law partner, George. The other is Phil.

Following the dissolution of our partnership, George continued practicing law, initially with one of our former associates, before eventually establishing his firm. Though our professional lives had diverged, we did cross paths, and I occasionally encountered him in the courthouse while volunteering as an ad litem, advocating for children in need of independent counsel. At first, there was still tension between us, but over time, we developed a new understanding where we could see past our differences and appreciate each other's virtues. In one of our final conversations, George shared a sobering message from his doctor: if he did not stop drinking, the damage to his liver would be irreversible.

We eventually lost touch. A year or two passed before one day, I found a note on my door. It was from the mother of George's third child. Her message was simple: "Call me," followed by her name and phone number. I called, and she shared the news: George had died. Despite our differences, the loss struck me deeply.

Her words brought to mind an interview I had once heard with the writer Philip Roth. When asked about aging, Roth noted that while we intellectually grasp the inevitability of death and expect to outlive those older than us, nothing prepares us for the death of our peers — our friends.[41] His observation rang painfully true. I was stunned.

George achieved much in his life. He was an Eagle Scout, a US Army pilot, and the holder of five advanced degrees, not to mention a passionate horseback rider. George and I had been more than friends. I had watched his children grow up; we built a firm together, tried cases together, each one representing a shared lifetime of its own, and even traveled together, visiting remote parts of the globe to fish. Nor was George one to stand down for anything, even at the time we were stopped and searched at gunpoint in a jungle. Yet, despite this storied life filled with accomplishments, there was one battle he could not win: his fight with alcohol.

Phil, the other instrumental figure in this story, also experienced a life-changing transformation. Within a year after our coaching sessions ended, he was ordained as a Zen priest in the Suzuki Roshi lineage. He retired from executive coaching and dedicated himself entirely to formal training. Tragically, his new chapter was short-lived. He was diagnosed with cancer soon after and died at the age of sixty-two. Just weeks before what he called his *transition*, a group of his former students, myself included, organized a call. With equanimity and grace, Phil shared his final lessons on love, grief, and the nature of change.

We recorded the conversation, and each year, I revisit it, discovering new layers of wisdom with every listen. Phil's teachings were simple but profound: Stay present, live purposefully, expand your awareness, release regrets, and practice unconditional love. These lessons remain as vivid today as they did in that last call. Phil's teachings endure not merely as isolated insights but as a golden thread woven through the lives of those he mentored. I am but one of many who continue to find inspiration in his insights, a testament to the sustaining influence of genuine wisdom.

As for my life today, I see now how clearly the choices of the past led to this point. Some were fleeting. Others lingered. At five: whether to borrow three dollars from my parents for a cowboy hat. At sixteen: whether to leave an unhealthy home. In my twenties: whether to undergo chemotherapy for cancer. Later: whether to attend law school in California or remain near the doctors who had saved my life. Each decision, these and others, carried something forward from one stage of life to the next. Taken together, they inform how I live and choose today.

Among these, the move into finance continues to manifest through my work. My career has become much of what I had hoped: collaborating with bright people, building businesses that meet real needs, and making a meaningful contribution. The early years were not without difficulty. There were days I felt like an imposter, and there are days I still do. And yet the labor continues, with its challenges, rewards, and daily opportunities to pursue, practice, and learn from others.

While wisdom remains at the forefront of my life, I continue to be a work in progress — with some days marked by forward motion and others by retreat. But one choice continues to haunt me: whether to dwell on my past mistakes or release the weight of regret.

And the evolution continues. Meanwhile, I recognize that my life holds no greater or lesser meaning than any other. We each write our story with uniquely cast roles. Like George and Phil, I have played a part in the lives of others, just as others have played a part in mine. Perhaps that is the best we can do — to offer one another a measure of insight, a measure of grace. I hope they found moments of wisdom in our time together, just as I did in knowing them.

I miss them both.

Acknowledgments

If there is anything of value in these pages, its origins lie in the presence and example of those who have illuminated my ways of thinking and being. Like stars scattered across a wide sky, each has cast a light — distinct, enduring — that has enlivened the wisdom in others, including me.

Among those whose brilliance I am especially grateful for are:

my friends and family, by origin and by choice, who remain a constant source of warmth and connection — a living reminder of what matters most

the men of my Tuesday Group, more than fifteen years on, for the insights, the challenge, the example you set, and most of all, your constant friendship

my colleagues at Satori Capital, who exemplify an exceptionally disciplined approach to decision-making in service of creating, funding, and inspiring businesses that elevate humanity

the Stagen Institute, for drawing together a community devoted to self-mastery, principled leadership, and the ongoing work of realizing the possible

the 5:30 a.m. workout crew, steadfast, outdoors, rain or shine — through more than a thousand shared sunrises, you have shown me that the first step toward transformation is showing up

the editors and proofreaders whose provocative questions, steady hands, and discerning eyes helped refine the work, word by word, faithful to its original intent

and the early readers whose patient reading and thoughtful responses provided the encouragement to bring this work to light.

Appendix A — The Wisdom Worksheet: A Quick Reference Guide

Within the pages of this book, you will discover a seven-step process to help you master the art of wise decision-making. Each chapter guides you through these steps with insights, personal anecdotes, and practical exercises to deepen your understanding. And yet, life happens. Decisions do not wait.

Whether you are confronting an important choice today, reflecting on decisions as you read, or seeking a refresher long after finishing this book, the Wisdom Worksheet is here for you. This quick reference guide can assist you at any time: as a tool to address immediate questions, as a complement to the chapters you are reading, or as a trusted resource for revisiting the process in the future. Both the seven questions and the example that follows are intended to provide inspiration and guidance as you consider the questions before you.

Feel free to return to this resource at any time, even before you have finished reading the book.

The Seven-Step Process for Making Better Decisions
Identify a question, issue, or dilemma you are facing or have been avoiding. Take the time — at least fifteen minutes — to examine it fully. Approach the matter with unwavering honesty. Once the right response emerges — and it will — commit to follow through.

Step 1: Ask the Question
Articulate the question clearly and concisely, ideally limiting the possible responses to two (e.g., whether to do A or B). Then, write it out.

Step 2: Acknowledge Your Immediate Response

A. After rereading the question, write out your initial (unfiltered) response.

B. List arguments in favor of and against acting on your initial response.

Step 3: Seek Perspective

A. Identify the people or groups most affected by your decision, then narrow your list to three to five and ask yourself: *What would each suggest?* If appropriate, ask them directly.

B. Assess the reliability of the response by evaluating their understanding of the context, your intentions, and any potential biases or personal interests.

C. What facts might they lack that would alter their advice?

Step 4: Envision Someone Wise

A. Picture a wise advisor — a figure you admire, an expert, a person you look to for guidance, or perhaps, the future, more experienced you.

B. What questions might they ask you?

Examples might include: What do you really desire? Will this matter in a year? What assumptions/stories are you telling yourself? What would you advise a friend in this situation? What is the larger question behind the question?

Step 5: Engage the Voice of Wisdom

Now pause.

Consider closing your eyes. (If this is your first time trying this, I encourage you to do so — it can help you focus and enhance the experience.)

Take a few deep breaths.

As you continue breathing deeply, shift your attention inward.

Locate the center of your being, the place where you feel relaxed, centered, and calm. (You may feel your muscles begin to slacken.)

Reconnect with the part of you that knows you — your fears, desires, intentions, aspirations. (The part of you that knows right from wrong and ensures your health, happiness, and success.)

Gently but firmly hold your attention here as you summon your awareness to this place. (Take your time; the question is already here.)

Continue to remain here, open and present, *listening* for whatever arises . . .

Though it may not utter a word or sound, the voice of wisdom will guide you.

To hear it is to experience an aha! — a subtle pull or inner knowing at the center of your being.

It will direct you toward the right thoughts, words, or actions.

You will know it is true when your body, heart, and mind confirm it.

While the answer may take time to make itself known, you will have initiated the process.

The right response will emerge in its own time and its own way.

Step 6: Act

Now that you know the right answer, what actions must you take? (This might involve accepting what is, taking a stand for change, moving in a new direction, or simply trusting yourself.)

Step 7: Observe and Adapt

The process does not end with one choice or action. Ongoing awareness ensures that you learn from your decisions so you can adapt and change — each right choice propelling you toward the future you desire.

Appendix B — The Wisdom Worksheet: Example Dilemma

The following example draws on themes and characters from *Romeo and Juliet*, a story that endures because it embodies the timeless struggle between loyalty and desire, duty and passion. At its core is Juliet's defining dilemma: a choice between fidelity to her family and the pursuit of a love that transcends the divisions of her community. This poignant conflict mirrors a universal dilemma — the tension between conforming to societal expectations and the pursuit of one's greatest dreams.

Step 1: Ask the Question

A. The question
- Should I (A) marry Romeo or (B) not marry Romeo?

Step 2: Acknowledge Your Immediate Response

A. Immediate response
- Marry Romeo — he is the one.

B. Arguments in favor of and against

For:
- Romeo is the love of my life.
- Marrying Romeo could free me from the looming threat of an arranged marriage to Paris.
- Our connection transcends family divisions.

Against:
- Romeo's family, the Montagues, are sworn enemies of my family, the Capulets.
- The marriage could escalate tensions, threatening peace in Verona.

Step 3: Seek Perspective

A. People or groups affected and their suggestions
- Romeo: "With love's light wings did I o'er perch these walls; For stony limits cannot hold [our] love out."[42]
- Capulets: "Now, by the stock and honour of my kin, to strike [Romeo] dead, I hold it not a sin."[43]
- Montagues: "Thou villain Capulet! — Hold me not; let me go."[44]
- Community: "If ever you disturb our streets again, Your lives shall pay the forfeit of the peace."[45]

B. Evaluating their thoughtfulness and reliability
- Romeo: His optimism reflects his love but underestimates the risks of defying the feud.
- Capulets: Their loyalty to family honor and pride dismisses the possibility of reconciliation or peace.
- Montagues: Their fiery hatred for the Capulets reflects a commitment to family honor at the expense of future generations.
- Community: Their value of peace is valid but may overlook the importance of personal freedom.

C. Facts they might lack:
- I seek to avoid an arranged marriage to Paris.
- I am drawn to the drama and defiance of a forbidden love.

Step 4: Envision Someone Wise

A. Wise advisor[46]
Friar Laurence: A trusted counselor who understands the surrounding circumstances, including the long-standing animosity between the Montagues and Capulets. Having known Juliet since she was a child, he has witnessed her love for Romeo firsthand. While not infallible, Friar Laurence is well-intentioned and values love, harmony, and peace, striving to bridge the divide between the families.

B. Questions he or she might ask
- How can your love for Romeo inspire reconciliation between your families?
- What actions could persuade both families to consent to or at least tolerate your union?
- Is there a way to express your love without risking harm to yourself and others?

Step 5: Engage the Voice of Wisdom

- Love conquers all — when built on a foundation of honesty and communication.
- If our families could see the love between us, they would consent to the marriage.
- Faking death merely avoids the difficult challenge rather than confronting it and fostering unity.

Step 6: Act

- I commit to openly demonstrating my love for Romeo and persisting in efforts to reconcile our families.
- Explore alternative ways to gain approval or seek support from neutral parties to bridge the divide.

Step 7: Observe and Adapt

Observation:
- Romeo and I failed to face adversity together, instead resorting to impulsive actions — faking our deaths.
- This reliance on deception led to tragic misunderstandings and irreversible consequences.
- Rather than finding a way forward, our choices ultimately cost us the chance at life and love.

Adaptation:
- Speak openly and truthfully with those I love, refraining from secrecy or deceit.
- Consider the long-term consequences of actions — avoiding rash decisions such as running away or resorting to violence.
- Enlist the support of trusted allies to mediate conflicts and work toward peace.

Notes

1   Paul B. Baltes and Ursula M. Staudinger, "Wisdom: A Metaheuristic (Pragmatic) to Orchestrate Mind and Virtue Toward Excellence," *American Psychologist* 55, no. 1 (2000): 122–36. See, for example, the Berlin Wisdom Project, initiated in the late 1970s at the Max Planck Institute, which studied wisdom as a system of expert knowledge addressing fundamental life questions.

2   Alfred Korzybski, *Science and Sanity: An Introduction to Non-Aristotelian Systems and General Semantics*, 5th ed. (Institute of General Semantics, 1994), xxv.

3   The skeptical part of me also questioned ecclesiastical faith over direct experience or the literal adherence to a book written decades after the protagonist's death in a regional dialect of Greek based on conflicting oral histories, themselves drawn from Hebrew and Aramaic. Besides, how was the Christian God any different than, say, Zeus, Jupiter, Ra, Vishnu, or Quetzalcoatl? Moreover, I had difficulty seeing past religion's unattractive shadows: dogmatic theology, discouragement of critical thinking, and exclusionary tribalism. Buddhism felt intellectually honest, encouraging doubt and self-determination.

4   Hermann Hesse, *Demian: The Story of Emil Sinclair's Youth*, trans. Michael Roloff and Michael Lebeck (Harper & Row, 1965).

5   T. S. Eliot, *The Rock: A Pageant Play* (Faber & Faber, 1934).

6   Hinduism: "The offering of wisdom is better than any material offering . . . for the goal of all work is spiritual wisdom." E. Easwaran, trans., "Wisdom in Action," chap. 4 in *The Bhagavad Gita*, 2nd ed. (Nilgiri Press, 2007), 33.

Buddhism: "Choose the path that leads to nirvana; avoid the road to profit and pleasure. Remember this always, O disciples of the Buddha, and strive always for wisdom." E. Easwaran, trans., "The Immature," chap. 5 in *The Dhammapada*, 2nd ed. (Nilgiri Press, 2007), 75.

Islam: "Our Lord, make a messenger of their own rise up from among them, to recite Your revelations to them, teach them the Scripture and wisdom, and purify them: You are the Mighty, the Wise." M. A. S. Abdel Haleem, trans., *The Qur'an*, 2:29 (Oxford University Press, 2004).

Judaism/Christianity: "Get wisdom; get insight: do not forget, nor turn away from the words of my mouth. Do not forsake her, and she will keep you; love her, and she will guard you." *The New Oxford Annotated Bible*, Proverbs 4.5–6 (Oxford University Press, 2018).

7   *The New Oxford Annotated Bible*, Proverbs 4.5–6 (Oxford University Press, 2018).

8   Middle English from Old French *philosophie*, by way of Latin from Greek *philosophia*, "love of wisdom."

9   "True, modern athletes are stronger, bigger, faster and more accomplished than those of the past, but this does not affect anyone's survival the way becoming a bigger, stronger, faster gazelle would. Taking all factors together, humans evolve through the metabolism of experience. That is, we absorb everything going on in our environment, and in some rather mysterious ways the next generation knows more and can do more than we can. When Einstein published his General Theory of Relativity, Bertrand Russell famously said that he was one of three people in the world who understood it. Now a bright high-school student can grasp Einstein's principles, if not his mathematics." Deepak Chopra, "Evolution of Wisdom," *Resurgence & Ecologist*, July/August 2007.

10   Brian Wansink and Jeffery Sobal, "Mindless Eating: The 200 Daily Food Decisions We Overlook," *Environment and Behavior* 39, no. 1 (January 1, 2007): 106–123, https://doi.org/10.1177/0013916506295573. Studies suggest the number of choices we make a day is in the tens of thousands, with more than two hundred relating to what we eat alone.

11   Ron Ashkenas, "How Trivial Decisions Will Impact Your Happiness," *Harvard Business Review*, December 13, 2010, https://hbr.org/2010/12/how-trivial-decisions-will-imp.

12   Napoleon Hill, chap. 1 in *Think and Grow Rich* (The Ralston Society, 1937).

13   "Each year, at least 8 million tonnes of plastics leak into the ocean — which is equivalent to dumping the contents of one garbage truck into the ocean every minute. . . . In a business-as-usual scenario, the ocean is expected to contain 1 tonne of plastic for every 3 tonnes of fish by 2025, and by 2050, more plastics than fish [by weight]." *The New Plastics Economy: Rethinking the Future of Plastics*, (World Economic Forum, January 2016), https://www3.weforum.org/docs/WEF_The_New_Plastics_Economy.pdf.

14   James Baldwin, "As Much Truth as One Can Bear," in *The Cross of Redemption: Uncollected Writings*, ed. Randall Kenan (Pantheon Books, 2010), 28.

15   R. Edward Freeman, *Strategic Management: A Stakeholder Approach* (Cambridge University Press, March 11, 2010).

16   Sheena S. Iyengar and Mark R. Lepper, "When Choice Is Demotivating: Can One Desire Too Much of a Good Thing?" *Journal of Personality and Social Psychology* 79, no. 6 (2000): 995–1006, https://doi.org/10.1037/0022-3514.79.6.995.

17   Viktor E. Frankl, *Man's Search for Meaning* (Pocket Books, 1985).

18   Kenneth A. Kiewra, "A Review of Note-Taking: The Encoding-Storage Paradigm and Beyond," *Educational Psychology Review* 1, no. 2 (1989): 147–72, https://doi.org/10.1007/bf01326640.

19   See, for example, Jane Austen, *Pride and Prejudice* (T. Egerton, 1813), where first impressions play a pivotal role in the development of character relationships, and Daniel Kahneman, *Thinking, Fast and Slow* (Farrar, Straus and Giroux, 2011), which examines the cognitive processes involved in forming initial judgments.

20   "From Benjamin Franklin to Jonathan Williams, Jr., 8 April 1779," *Founders Online*, National Archives and Records Administration, accessed May 7, 2020, https://founders.archives.gov/documents/Franklin/01-29-02-0240. [Original source: Benjamin Franklin, "From Benjamin Franklin to Jonathan Williams, Jr., 8 April 1779," *The Papers of Benjamin Franklin* (Yale University Press, 1992)].

21   Charles Darwin, "Darwin on Marriage," *Darwin Correspondence Project*, Cambridge University Library, June 5, 2015, http://www.darwinproject.ac.uk/tags/about-darwin/family-life/darwin-marriage. [Original source: Frederick Burkhardt et al., *The Correspondence of Charles Darwin, Volume 2* (Cambridge University Press, 1987), 444].

22   Sigmund Freud, *The Basic Writings of Sigmund Freud*, ed. and trans. A. A. Brill (Modern Library, 1938).

23   F. Scott Fitzgerald, "The Crack-Up," *Esquire*, February 1, 1936.

24   Thomas C. Schelling, *Strategies of Commitment and Other Essays* (Harvard University Press, 2006). Thomas Schelling, Nobel laureate, Harvard professor for more than thirty years, co-founder of the Kennedy School at Harvard, game theorist, and inspiration for the Stanley Kubrick film *Dr. Strangelove or: How I Learned to Stop Worrying and Love the Bomb*, famously wrote, "One thing a person cannot do, no matter how rigorous his analysis or heroic his imagination, is to draw up a list of things that would never occur to him."

25   Aristotle, "Metaphysics," in *The Complete Works of Aristotle*, trans. W. D. Ross, ed. Jonathan Barnes (Princeton University Press, 1984), Book Alpha, 982b12-27.

26   Mencius, chap. 6 in *Mencius*, trans. D. C. Lau (Penguin Books, 1970).

27   Martin Heidegger, *Being and Time*, trans. John Macquarrie and Edward Robinson (Harper & Row, 1962). Originally published in 1927.

28   Nicholas Epley, *Mindwise: Why We Misunderstand What Others Think, Believe, Feel, and Want* (Vintage Books, 2015).

29   The Fat Buddha, also known as the Laughing Buddha, refers to a monk said to have lived around the tenth century CE. His real name, Budai, literally means *cloth sack*, referencing the bag he carries with him. Due to his ever-present smile and love of food and drink, he is often referred to as the Laughing Buddha or Fat Buddha, especially in the Western world. See, for example, "Laughing Buddha," *Tibetan Buddhist Encyclopedia*, accessed January 25, 2025, https://www. tibetanbuddhistencyclopedia.com/en/index.php?title=Laughing_Buddha.

30   Though its precise wording does not appear in any of the existing dialogues written by his student Plato, this quote summarizes Socratic philosophy as recorded in Plato's dialogues, particularly in *Apology*, where Socrates discusses his awareness of his own ignorance. See Plato, *Apology*, in *The Dialogues of Plato*, trans. Benjamin Jowett (Random House, 1937), 21–22.

31   Virtues can manifest in healthy or unhealthy ways. Consider compassion: Healthy compassion means empathizing with others' pain while maintaining healthy boundaries. You offer support and understanding without becoming overwhelmed or losing sight of your own needs. In contrast, unhealthy compassion involves getting so entangled in the suffering of others that you lose your own sense of self. This can lead to burnout, resentment, or enabling negative behaviors. Similarly, ambition can be a driving force for achievement, but an unhealthy manifestation might involve ruthlessly prioritizing success over personal relationships or disregarding ethical boundaries.

32   Mahatma Gandhi, *All Men Are Brothers: Life and Thoughts of Mahatma Gandhi as Told in His Own Words*, ed. Krishna Kripalani (Navajivan Publishing House, 1953).

33   John Swenson, ed., *The Rolling Stone Jazz Record Guide* (Random House, 1985).

34   Henry David Thoreau, *The Writings of Henry David Thoreau: Journal, March 2, 1859 to November 30, 1859*, ed. Bradford Torrey, vol. 12 (Boston: Houghton Mifflin and Company, 1906), 39.

35   Adapted from "The enemy has outnumbered and surrounded us on all sides. Now we can shoot them from every direction. Our victory is assured," attributed to Colonel Lewis B. "Chesty" Puller during the Chosin Reservoir campaign in Korea, November 1950. Quoted in Burke Davis, *Marine! The Life of Lt. Gen Lewis B. (Chesty) Puller, USMC (Ret.)* (Little, Brown and Company, 1962).

36   While Megginson was interpreting the ideas of Charles Darwin, the quote is often misattributed to Charles Darwin. Leon C. Megginson, "Lessons from Europe for America" (presidential address delivered at the Southwestern Social Science Association convention in San Antonio, Texas, April 12, 1963), *Southwestern Social Science Quarterly* 44, no. 1 (June 1963).

37   Charles Dickens, *A Christmas Carol* (Chapman & Hall, 1843), 25–26.

38   Plato, *The Republic*, trans. Benjamin Jowett (Vintage Books, 1991).

39   "Most men are satisfied if they read or hear, and perchance have been convicted by the wisdom of one good book, the Bible, and for the rest of their lives vegetate and dissipate their faculties in what is called easy reading. Henry David Thoreau, *Walden; or, Life in the Woods* (Ticknor and Fields, 1854).

40   Carl G. Jung, *Alchemical Studies: Volume 13 of The Collected Works of C. G. Jung*, trans. and ed. Gerhard Adler and R. F. C. Hull (Princeton University Press, 1967).

41   "If you're lucky, your grandparents will die when you're, say, in college. Mine died when I was a schoolboy. If you're lucky, your parents will live until you're somewhere in your 50's; if you're very lucky, into your 60's. You won't ever die, and your children, certainly, will never die before you. That's the deal, that's the contract. But in this contract nothing is written about your friends, so when they start dying, it's a gigantic shock." Charles McGrath, "Philip Roth, Haunted by Illness, Feels Fine," *New York Times*, April 25, 2006, https://www.nytimes.com/2006/04/25/books/philip-roth-haunted-by-illness-feels-fine.html.

42   William Shakespeare, *Romeo and Juliet*, act 2, scene 2, line 66.

43   William Shakespeare, *Romeo and Juliet*, act 1, scene 5, line 58.

44   William Shakespeare, *Romeo and Juliet*, act 1, scene 1, line 78.

45   William Shakespeare, *Romeo and Juliet*, act 1, scene 1, lines 91–92.

46   In the original story, Friar Laurence proposes drastic actions, including the secret marriage and ultimately the faked death, hoping these plans would reconcile the feuding families. However, these solutions rely heavily on chance and secrecy, leading to tragedy when communication fails. This underscores that even our wisest counsel can be fallible and highlights the importance of engaging the voice of wisdom.

www.ingramcontent.com/pod-product-compliance
Lightning Source LLC
Chambersburg PA
CBHW071845090426
42811CB00035B/2326/J